Displacement and Rehabilitation

Protest Movement Against Industrial Displacement in An Indian State

Displacement and Rehabilitation

Protest Movement Against Industrial Displacement in An Indian State

Niranjan Pani

Sandhya Rani Nayak

Pranab Choudhury

KALPAZ

ISBN: 978-93-5128-214-3

Price: ₹ 950/-

First Published, 2016

Published by

Kalpaz Publications
C-30, Satyawati Nagar,
Delhi – 110052
E-mail: kalpaz@hotmail.com
Ph.: 9212142040

Printed at: G. Print Process, Delhi

Cataloging in Publication Data–DK

Courtesy: D.K. Agencies (P) Ltd. <docinfo@dkagencies.com>

Suresh, Devath, author.

Development, displacement and rehabilitation : with special reference to tribal habitations of Andhra Pradesh / Dr Devath Suresh.

pages cm

Includes bibliographical references.

ISBN 9789351282136

1. Andhra Pradesh (India)--Scheduled tribes--Relocation. 2. Andhra Pradesh (India)--Scheduled tribes--Rehabilitation--Government policy. 3. Economic development projects--Social aspects--India--Andhra Pradesh. I. Title.

HB2100.A53S87 2016 DDC 304.808694095485 23

Contents

Chapter 1

Beginning

Recently National Human Rights Commission (NHRC)[1] issued a notice to Government of Odisha seeking its responses on alleged Human Rights violations in forceful displacement of 3000 families for Kanpur Irrigation Project on Baitarani River in Keonjhar. No doubt 'Displacement' for 'Development' is a sensitive issue. India's current development experience has been an astonishing success. The economy is in a strong position and is the fastest growing in the world. The high economic growth has largely remained confined to big cities, with the differences in the standard of living between the urban and rural areas are widening. It has meant slight to the poor of India including SCs, STs, OBCs and some minorities in rural areas. Mostly large-scale development projects in India have been planned and executed through a centralised, hierarchical and capital-intensive approach, which has assumed that technology has the answer to all development problems. As a result, project authorities have adopted a centralised 'command and control' system for administering and managing all stages of a project cycle. The approaches, techniques and systems, which were perhaps suitable for construction and mechanical production, were applied thoughtlessly to human communities. The Ministry of Water Resources, for example, may have the physical, mechanical or engineering skills to construct a 260 meters tall gigantic dam for impounding the river Bhagirathi, but it has never bothered to develop the skills and techniques required for relocating 85,000 mountain dwelling people and rehabilitating them in the plains at even the minimum levels of satisfaction. It is true that such deficiencies in development projects have been encountered in practically all countries, which have adopted large-scale projects without adequate investments in human resources or without assessing the accompanying human trauma adequately. Even more, it is necessary to critically examine the approach to development projects and ensuing phenomenon of displacement. Further, it has become almost a topmost priority to discover alternative ways of resettling and rehabilitating displaced people. Ideally, the process of development should generate benefits and opportunities for all, not accentuate the gaps already existing between the rich and the poor, and across regions and states.

Displacement is not politically neutral. It arises out of a clash of ideologies, on one side, the value systems of traditional cultures, where relationships with land and community are important than money, another side, an ideology of industrialisation-as-development, in which market forces and swift financial profit override other values. It has been argued that state has always served the interests of industrial capital. Modern state has been an instrument of large scale industrialisation that has alienated the people from their own natural resources. Displacement in Odisha is primarily due to large projects which cover not only industry but also mining, dams, industry, wildlife sanctuaries, Special Economic Zones and defence establishments. In this road to more and faster, we tend to forget the people who suffer from this race and are excluded from the process. Today's displacement is the result of policies of liberalisation, privatisation and globalisation. Globalisation is not a new phenomenon but its history can be linked to imperialism and western nation's search for more markets and primary goods. Displacement, it is observed, is almost always forced and not voluntary. The United Nations Guiding Principles on Internal Displacement based upon existing international humanitarian law and human rights instruments, which serve as an international standard to guide governments in providing assistance and protection to Internally Displaced Persons (IDPs), is rarely followed.

The issue of displacement is seen as necessary evil in order to construct industries, infrastructure such as dams, mining, roads, and power projects, which are intended to serve "greater good". The study will only focus on the issue of involuntary displacement in India. The drive for land acquisition on the name of modernisation and development has been the reason behind rise in protests by the farmers and tribal people across the country. The focus on economic issues overlook other no less important social and cultural issues, which may proved to be crucial in building links and networks in the new environment. The protests by civil society and peoples against land acquisition have been growing in recent years. The recent protest in Bhatta-Parsaul of Noida in Uttar Pradesh state tells us another centre of violence provoked by an attempt to displace the farmers. In fact, whether it is Kalinga Nagar in Odisha, Bhatta-Parsaul in UP, Nandigram in West Bengal, or other places in Chattisgarh, Jharkhand, Andrha Pradesh, Kerala, Tamil Nadu etc., all point the need to examine the matter immediately.

An important factor for development-induced displacement has been attributed as the approach taken towards development. Unfortunately, since independence, over the years of planned development, the government has assumed a dominant role in the process of development leading to the impoverishment of a large section of the population. One of the major concerns with such development projects has been that, very few amongst those displaced were resettled. Some projects formulated a Resettlement and Rehabilitation (R&R) Package for the project affected persons, however, in most cases the approaches adopted for resettlement have been found to be ineffective. There are two types of discussions taking place on this issue namely: those who argue for faster economic growth and others focus on the issues of environmental protection. There is a need to understand the choices to be made especially large projects that are considered crucial to economic growth but are detrimental to ecology and environment. India's economic liberalisation also known as New Economic Policy was launched in 1991. The major policy change was growth centered focus. It did not make any reference to long standing problems of the Indian economy such as poverty, malnutrition, unemployment, ill health, illiteracy and environmental degradation etc. However, Indian economy is predominantly rural in character. This is evidenced from the fact that in 2011, about 74 per cent of its population lived in some half million villages. India's two-third workforce is engaged in agricultural sector, and this sector contributed about 26 per cent of the GDP in 2009. Since the adoption of neoliberal reforms, the foreign investors have increased their presence in India. And various collaboration and joint ventures projects have been launched. For example, in recent years as many as 341 SEZs have been approved and set up across India. On the name of efficiency in agriculture sector, the World Bank and mainstream economists support increased capital intervention and commoditisation of land. For instance, the World Bank (2010) argues in favour of large scale land acquisition as a way to reduce poverty. The Bank suggests that large-scale land acquisition can be a vehicle for poverty reduction. The report further suggests that increased private capital investment in agriculture will create more jobs and new opportunities for contract farmers. There are various examples of large scale mechanised production of soya and grains in North America and Argentina. The study notes, "near-industrial methods of quality control and production at low cost, managed by high quality agronomists using land leased by corporations that pay high rents for land, making it advantages for landholder to cease their own production. The report does not provide any concrete evidence of job creation due to increased mechanisation in large farms. It would like to see reversal of land reforms in developing countries. It seems that the only success criteria are efficiency and profits. The study favours a laissez-faire approach in which private investors take command from small and medium farmers into contract farmers arguing that, "productivity and welfare enhancing transactions can occur without the need for active intervention by the state". Contrary to the Bank's claims, in various developing countries, it is found that the influx of capital in agriculture did not result into job creation; it rather widened rural inequality and increased involvement of private capital. No jobs were created to affected people, as initially claimed. In fact, the World Bank's led 'Structural Adjustment Programmes (also known as neoliberal reforms) were launched in the developing countries during the 1980s. Thanks to these reforms that subsidies to agriculture sector were withdrawn and private investment was to replace public investment, along with the removal to trade and investment in the developing countries.

Simultaneously, development has its flipsides too; displacement, being one of the most painful and cruel effect. Displacement can be development induced, or through natural disasters like floods, droughts, earthquakes and cyclones. There is also process-induced displacement such as those caused by the introduction of new technologies as in the example of trawlers in fishing. Displacement may be voluntary or involuntary migration caused by wars and other upheavals in society or the displacement of tribal through land alienation and eviction of non-tribals encroaches in the reserve forests.

Acquisition of agricultural land for industrial purposes in India is not new. Heavy industrialisation is at the core of India's planned development and hence large areas had to be acquired. The proximity to market-cum-physical infrastructure for location of industries means people settled by housing are to be displaced. While landowners give up land in the process of acquisition by the State, landless people are deprived twice, once by not getting the opportunity to work on land as agricultural labourers and the second time by not being in the net of compensation. Obviously, the landless people are mainly dependent on Common Property Resources (CPRs) and are outside the purview of compensation of any type. The land area required, in turn, is directly proportional to the type of projects undertaken. Some examples are cited below:

(i) POSCO, the world's fourth largest South Korean steel company, had signed a MoU with the Government of Odisha in 2005 to set up a plant, near Paradip Port in Odisha's Jagatsinghpur District that will produce 12 million tons of steel per annum. Approx. 3,000 families were to be displaced. The people, resisting land acquisition, opined that the project would destroy their livelihood that thrives on shrimp farming and cultivation of betel leaves, a highly profitable crop. They rejected the rehabilitation package for the displaceable, announced by the Odisha Government.

(ii) In the power sector, the NTPC Ltd. and Uttar Pradesh Rajya Vidyut Nigam Ltd. (UPRVNL), on the 22 November 2007 signed a Memorandum of Understanding (MoU) to set up a thermal power plant of 1,320 MW at Kohrarghat of Meha Tehsil in Allahabad District of east UP. The government of UP acquired a total land area of 2500 acres for setting up the plant that affected the livelihood of 469 settled households. This adversely affected agricultural output and food security.

(iii) To set up a 3500 MW gas-based power plant with an estimated project cost of Rs 25,000 cr in Dadri Region in Ghaziabad District, Hapur Tehsil, in western UP, the Government of Uttar Pradesh acquired about 1,011 hectare of land in the year 2004. Most of the land acquired was earlier used for agricultural purposes. The major assets covered in land acquisition were canals, ponds and wells. Land acquisition in Dadri was estimated to have led to displacement of over 6,000 families.

Further to make the book a comprehensive one the highlighted objectives are : (a) To analyse the major factors that lead to displacement and its positive and negative impacts; (b) To examine the prevalence of the Rehabilitation Policies work; (c) To focus and analyse the steps taken by the government for the resettlement of the displaced people; (d) To explore the impact of globalisation and liberalisation on the industrial development and displacement; (e) To place an opinion study of respondents and; (f) To provide a concluding remark on the rehabilitation policy in India indicating suggestive improvements in the area. Also to add to it four core hypotheses are taken for testing. The very purpose of it is to fortify the study. As a matter of fact the hypotheses are: (1) Though Odisha's draft resettlement and rehabilitation policy is an improvement on the national policy, it does not go far enough in ensuring adequate majors to the affected people; (2) The development-induced –displacement process is leading to widening the gap between the rich and poor; (3) The present pattern of development is the continuing powerlessness of the weaker sections due to displacement and without any benefits from these development projects; and (4) The Rehabilitation policy promises for the betterment of ousters but actually the effect is impoverishment, landlessness, joblessness, food insecurity, loss of common property and increased mortality.

Besides, the present study maintained the theoretical prospective as an important constraint in guiding the research into the problem and followed a systematic method in analysing and interpreting the material available in the field. For data collection the scholar has interviewed 500 respondents. For this purpose scientific methods comprising of survey and questionnaire techniques are used. Here four square stratified random sampling was used. The whole nucleus was stratified into industrial displaced persons of different parts of

Odisha. Among the stratified groups, questionnaire groups are adopted for collection of primary data randomly. Statistical techniques like X^{2-} test, rank analysis, correlation etc, have been used to justify the strength of the obtained results. The results have been obtained by using IBM SPSS 20.0 package which is widely used and acclaimed software. The questionnaire consists of 27 questions. Out of 500 respondents, 20 respondents have no knowledge about Rehabilitation Policy of Government. Hence, their responses are ignored while analysing the data. Effectively the nucleus (n) of the data is 480. The study being contemporary in nature has followed both historical and analytical method. Different books and articles of this field are used as secondary sources. Articles written by eminent scholar were of great use and served as an important source of information for the work.

Above all the study will be a guide for Resentment Movements against Displacement in India, as the study will try to explore the whole gamut of the problem from all angles. Moreover administrators, planners, scholars and general readers will also benefit much from the study. The study will be a guide for rehabilitation policy in India and Odisha as the scholar will try to explore the scope of the problem from all angles.

Note

1. Reported in Times of India, Bhubaneswar, December 14, 2015.

Chapter 2

Rehabilitation Policy: India Context

According to UN guiding principles on Internal Displacement, 'Internally displaced persons are persons or groups of persons who have been forced or obliged to flee or to leave their homes or places of habitual residence, in particular as a result of or in order to avoid the effects of armed conflict, situations of generalised violence, violations of human rights, natural or human-made disasters, and who have not crossed an internationally recognised State border.' India has invested in industrial projects, dams, roads, mines, power plants and new cities to achieve rapid economic growth. This has been made possible through massive acquisition of land and subsequent displacement of people. Development Displacement Population is the single largest category among all Internally Displaced Populations (IDPs). In India around 50 million people have been displaced due to development projects in over 50 years. Around 21.3 million development-induced IDPs include those displaced by dams (16.4 million), mines (2.55 million), industrial development (1.25 million) and wildlife sanctuaries and national parks (0.6 million).[1]

Studies of displacement and deprivation have been conducted in Odisha, Jharkhand, Andhra Pradesh, Kerala, Goa, West Bengal and Assam. These studies show that displacement is high. For example, Assam has 1,909,368 DP/PAPs from 1,401,184.8 acres and West Bengal has 6,944,492 from 4,764,000 acres. With data from ongoing studies, they point to an all-India figure of 60 million DP/PAPs (Displaced Person/Project affected Persons) during the period 1947-2000 from 25 million ha, including 7 million ha of forests and 6 million ha of other CPRs. For example officially, Assam has used 392,773 acres of land for development projects and has caused 343,262 DP/PAPs.

Large-scale development projects in India have been planned and executed through a centralised, hierarchical and capital-intensive approach, which has assumed that technology has the answer to all development problems. As a result, project authorities have adopted a centralised 'command and control' system for administering and managing all stages of a project cycle. The approaches, techniques and systems, which were perhaps suitable for construction and mechanical production, were applied thoughtlessly to human communities. The Ministry of Water Resources, for example, may have the physical, mechanical or engineering skills to construct a 260 meters tall gigantic dam for impounding the river Bhagirathi, but it has never bothered to develop the skills and techniques required for relocating 85,000 mountain dwelling people and rehabilitating them in the plains at even the minimum levels of satisfaction.

The past few decades have witnessed rapid economic growth in the country and the process forms a part of 'planned development'. This is manifested in the setting up of large-scale projects in power generation, mining, industry, infrastructure development, irrigation and even in creating new urban settlements. This involves large-scale land acquisition and even demolition of homesteads. India presents great variance in terms of development-induced displacement. However, large dams are the single largest cause of displacement in India since independence. The World Bank notes that though large dams constitute only 26.6 per cent of the total World Bank funded projects causing displacement, the resulting displacement makes up 62.8 per cent of the total number of people displaced[2]. Displacement now-a-days is not a very unfamiliar name while discussing about various developmental projects. But serious concern is that displacement is expanding its size and its adverse impacts on the innocent people who are sacrificing a lot including their own habitat for the development project. In India around 50 million people have been displaced in the last 50 years for various development projects. But the sad thing is that most of them have never been properly resettled. Prior to 1990s displacement tremor is mostly confined to tribal and rural areas because most of the displacement cases were resulted from big dams. But after the era of globalisation the Indian economy changed a lot. Many MNCs are entering Indian market. So displacement on a large scale is now increasingly occurring by other kinds of projects like thermal power stations, mining, steel industries, manufacturing industries, automobile industries, highways, airports, ports and urban development.

After globalisation the private sector has emerged as a major player in the development process. To achieve higher economic growth target various State Governments are trying to attract private investment in different sectors like power generation, manufacturing, mining, steel, roads, airports etc. Special Economic Zone (SEZs) for large private corporations of India (like Reliance, Tata etc.) and also for multinational Corporations (MNC's) are being set up to accelerate the development process. Due to the pressure of Globalisation various laws are amended to make them investor friendly regardless of what happens to the livelihoods of farmers whose land will be gone for the project. Another major factor is India's population. The population of India is growing very rapidly. 'India is going to be the most populated country in near future. India's population is growing more in one week than the entire European Union's population grows during a full year.[3] Due to this the Land Human Ratio will worsen more. Due to the high population density, it will not be easy to start a project without displacing huge number of people even in remote areas. A Study of dam projects from Odisha explains that during 1950s the number of person displaced per hectare was 1.9. But it increases to 5.52 during 1980[4].

The past knowledge of resettlement has shown that people who are displaced due to such development projects do not improve from their previous standard of living. Resettlement studies have brightly documented the devastating consequences of failed resettlement projects which inspite of improving the standard of living of displaced people, creates new pockets of poverty. So for the displaced persons development has been too often experienced not as an opportunity but as disruption and impoverishment. Sometimes displacement not only puts affected people to grave impoverishment risk but also causes a setback to the poverty reduction effort. Resettlement studies have also shown that the poor who are most at risk always suffer the most and ends up poorer than before. The affluent group gets most of the benefits all the time. The affluent group turns displacement into an opportunity by which they can become richer. Using their power and money the rich are quick to seize various benefits that the projects generate. An example from the Tehri Dam Project where in connivance with the project officials the rich people hurriedly built some 5000 bogus houses in the submergence zone, declared these as long established family properties, and got away with hefty amounts as compensation claims. The only people who did not get any benefit were the real oustees, in spite of the resettlement promises. The poor not only lose their land due to displacement but also lose their basic human rights. Very often they are not consulted during the project planning process though it is their lives that are most directly affected by the project. Often they don't know when will they get the compensation and how much will they get as compensation. Many times relocation is carried out by coercive methods. Any resistance to relocation is suppressed by using brute force. Protest against the threat of displacement is suppressed with police firing. 12 tribal people died on the spot when police opened fire on a crowd protesting over land acquisition for the construction of a steel plant in Kalinga Nagar Industrial Complex in Jajpur District on January 2006 of Odisha. The Government of West Bengal also uses police force to suppress the protest by people. Many people died by the police firing in Singur where Tata's Nano Project was scheduled to established earlier. Police also fired on people protesting against a SEZ to be established by for a foreign Company at Nandigram.

Though Development projects were undertaken to promote wider social development, seldom the displaced person is the beneficiary of development projects. The benefits mostly go to an entirely different set of people who are not affected by the project. Very often those who receive the benefits usually are urban dwellers, commercial farmers etc. and not the group that bear the social cost. For example electricity is generated at Rengali Dam area of Odisha. But the benefit goes to urban centers and industries located hundreds of miles away. The poor people in that region who gave up their land are still poor and have no access to electricity. Due to Development projects some people gain and some loose. This gives rise to a conflicting situation.

The major source of the conflict lies in the inequitable sharing of project benefits. Generally powerful group gains from projects and justify displacement in the name of national interest. While the poor group those who are adversely affected are portrayed as obstacles in the path of development. In the early days of planned development projects, seldom there was opposition to projects. People in the early ages used to believe that development will bring prosperity to all. For this reason, they provide their land for development projects easily. Farmers take whatever cash compensation was given to them and then move on to resettle at somewhere else. But the scenario has changed now a day, People are more aware about their rights and laws. The media is also very powerful. Poor people who will be displaced due to a development project could know what has happened to the displaced people of other projects. How they are resettled, where they are resettled and what is their social, mental and financial condition in the new place. Due to media, protests started in unknown villages are becoming issues of global concern. For example Narmada Bachao Andolan, Protest against POSCO in an unknown village called Dhinkia, Protest against Tatas in Kalinga Nagar are topics of international debate. The protestors are also getting support from the human rights activities group. The increased media attention to these protests also helping the protestors many a time.

Development projects that involve displacement of people from their lands and livelihoods have long been the subject of major controversies but in recent years the issue has become particularly controversial. There are various groups that not only oppose the poor resettlement out comes that cause widespread impoverishment, but denounce the entire development approach as destructive and demand that no development programme that involves displacement should be under taken. Though concern to save poor people from the adverse effects of development-induced displacement is legitimate, the demand for stopping all development projects is truly unrealistic and impossible. The number of those who will be displaced and resettled can be reduced by thoughtful project designing. The fact is that projects that often cause displacement are needed to promote development and improve living condition for all.

Types of Displacement

There are different types of Displacement—

(1) **Voluntary Migrants** – Some people migrate from their home voluntarily in search of employment, better job, better life style and better prospects. Those people are called as voluntary migrants.

(2) **Refugees** – Some people are forced to move out of their habitat by wars and civil unrest. That type of people care called Refugees. For exam: around 15 to 20 million persons migrated from India to Pakistan or from Pakistan to India during the partition of India in 1947.

(3) **Disaster Refugees** – Due to natural and sometimes man-made disasters many people are forced to leave their own land. For ex: Many people leave their habitat in Jagatsinghpur area of Odisha due to super cyclone. Due to Tsunami many people are forced to leave their habitat. One example of man-made disaster is Bhopal gas tragedy due to which many people leave their own land.

(4) **Processed Displaced Persons** – Sometimes people leave their land when they loose their livelihood due to some changes introduced in the economy in their areas. For Exam: traditional fishing families were affected when trawlers were allowed in shallow waters.

(5) **Displaced Persons** – Displaced persons (DPs) are those persons who are displaced due to land displacement. The displaced persons are those who are forced to move out of their land when the development projects require acquisition of their homesteads.

(6) **Project Affected People** – Project Affected People (PAP) are people whose livelihood is alienated from them though they may remain where they are. The PAPs are those who loose their livelihood and assets fully or partially without being displaced. In some case their individual land is acquired and in others, the common properly like forests fishing areas which are their livelihoods are acquired. This is graphically presented below (Figure 2.1).

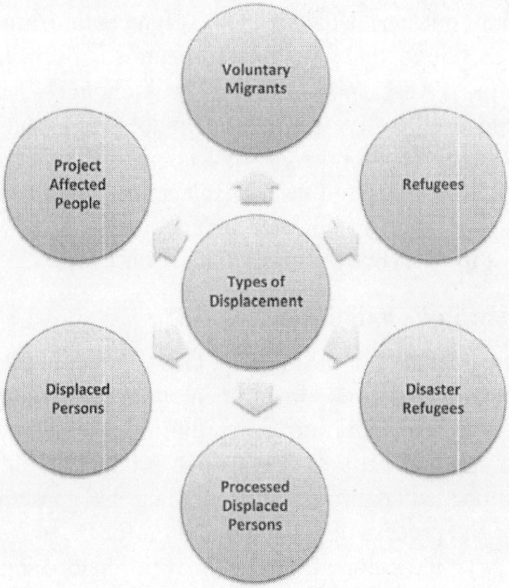

Figure 2.1 : Types of Displacement

Development Induced Displacement in India: Backdrop

In the early 80s resentment movement against Hirakud Dam in Odisha attracted wide public attention throughout India. In the 1990s the Sardar Sarovar Dam Project in Gujarat and Tehri Dam in Uttarakhand were on focus of people. Though resentment movement against displacement in Kalinga Nagar (TATA), Dhinkia (POSCO), Singur (TATA) are on headlines and breaking news, such struggle exist all over India. Protest against SEZs in Mavi Mumbai, Gujarat, Haryana, Mining and Steel industries in different parts of Chhattisgarh, Jharkhand and Odisha are gaining momentum. This symbolised the change brought by globalisation. With Profit as sole criterion the corporate sector is demanding more land than they used to do in the past. This is causing more development induced displacement.

Displacement in Early Ages

Displacement due to development projects is not new in India. There are signs that suggest displacement due to development also occurred in Gupta dynasty. In the middle ages projects such as Jai

Samand Lake built near Udaipur in the eighteenth century affected many families.[5] But at that time displacement is not very harmful. As the population is very small and land was enough, the displaced persons could used to live nearer to a place from where they are displaced. Resettlement for those displaced persons near their original habitat is not a very difficult task. Displacement became an issue in the colonial age, intensified after independence and is providing serious threat to everybody after globalisation.

Displacement in Colonial Age

The main objective of the colonial Government is profit. Hence, the objective of the colonial Government after Industrial Revolution in England is to turn India into a supplier of capital, raw material, labour force and make it a market for the products. So the colonial Government opened coal mines in Rani Ganj, tea gardens in Assam etc. To make the process of land Acquisition for the above purposes at a lowest price the colonial Government introduced legal changes and Land Acquisition Act, 1894 was brought up.

Displacement in Pre Independence India

Many people object to the importance given to the rights of Displaced people (DPs) for Resettlement and Rehabilitation. But the true fact is that this phenomenon is therefor centuries without a systematic approach to Resettlement and Rehabilitation. In many other areas of human society, consciousness about their consequences has grown only in recent years. The negative impact of displacement in pre independence India is minimal since land is abundant and the population density was small. As a result of which the Displaced Persons and Projected Affected People could resettle themselves in a new place with limited problems. But the problem touches the alarm under the British rule and intensified further after independence because of planned development.

The process of enacting the Land Acquisition Act began with the permanent settlement Act, of 1793 in an effort to ensure regular land tax collection. The British Government handed over large area of land to the zamindars, who collected land tax. Due to this many farmers lost their land. The British Government tried to take control of large area of land with the help of another act (Assam Land Act,

1834) whose main purpose was to get as much land as possible at a very low price for tea estates. Calcutta Law of 1824 is implemented to acquire land for the purpose of salt pans. Freedom fighter Dadabhai Naraji estimated that around 35 million people were deprived of their livelihood as a result of the British policy. These changes turned a large number of landless agricultural labours to cheap labour. They were transported as indentured labour in slave like conditions to plantations and mines in India and other British colonies. While many surrender to the situation some others resisted which led to struggle against displacement. One example is Mulsipeta struggle near Pune in 1920.

In the colonial age the British Government tried to develop the British economy at the cost of Indian economy. So the British Government tried to change the Indian economy to suit the needs of the British Industrial Revolution. It required raw materials like cotton and tea and the money to fund it. So the British Government turns India into a supplier of capital and raw materials for the development of Britain. In order to procure these raw materials the British Government needed to acquire as much land as possible for projects like coalmines, coffee and tea estates, Railways and roads. Various efforts are made in the form of enactment of new land laws so as to transfer land to British mining and plantation companies. All these efforts resulted the Land Acquisition Act, (LAA 1894). The changes in the land laws were integral to the British Government effort in maximising its gain from India.

Displacement in Post Independence Era

Due to Land Acquisition Act, 1894 displacement remain arbitrary even today. It allows the state to displace people without their consent and without specifying the nature of the public purpose for doing so. So many socialists argues that the post independence thinking on development is not very different from the motive of the colonialist as most projects give priority to economic efficiency and do not give much importance to well being of the people affected by them. After independence many Indian leaders who completed their education abroad took the responsibility of development of India to their shoulder. They had seen the progress made by technologically advanced and industrialised countries of west. They attributed this progress to technology alone. But some leaders including Mahatma Gandhi were able to see that the western colonising nations had become rich by exploiting their colonies. So Mahatma Gandhi cautioned the independent India against following the western pattern of development. He did not oppose industrialisation but oppose industrialism. He opposed the development based on the types of technology and consumption patterns that were expected to be beyond the reach of majority. At that time many leaders and national planners viewed development mainly as economic growth. This thinking was prevalent in the Bombay plan, 1945 which was prepared by a group of Indian entrepreneurs. It recommended that since the Indian private sector lacked resources to invest in infrastructure like steel and power which would yield profit in long run, the infrastructure should be built by the state with the taxpayer's money. The profitable consumer sector should be left to private investor. This recommendation was accepted in 1956 as mixed economy and is reflected in the second five year plan 1956-57 to 1960-61.

This thought patterns about development, developed in India during the latter half of the twentieth century resulted in industrial projects based on sophisticated projects. Priority was given to massive dams like Hirakud in Odisha, Nagarjuna and Tungabhadra in Andhra Pradesh, Bhakra Nangal in Himachal Pradesh and Damodar valley in Jharkhand. Others included steel plants, heavy electrical, machine tools etc. even Jawaharlal Nehru the then Prime Minister of India declared at the inauguration of Hirakud dam that such projects were the temple of modern India. Heavy infrastructure was needed to give shape to these types of gigantic projects. Western colonising nations could afford extensive use of these resources because much of their raw materials was brought from their colonies. India is a thickly populated country does not have much land to spare. As the focus of development activities is on economic growth, the social sector continues to be neglected. As a result little attention has been paid to the consequences of economic growth-oriented development activities which are causing large scale displacement of people, particularly of those living in rural and tribal areas.

Features of Post-independence development

Displacement intensified after 1951 due to various development projects coming into act. At that time India doesn't have a rehabilitation act or law. So it is not possible to work out the exact nature of displacement in terms of numbers and types. Some of the features of post independences displacement are placed below:

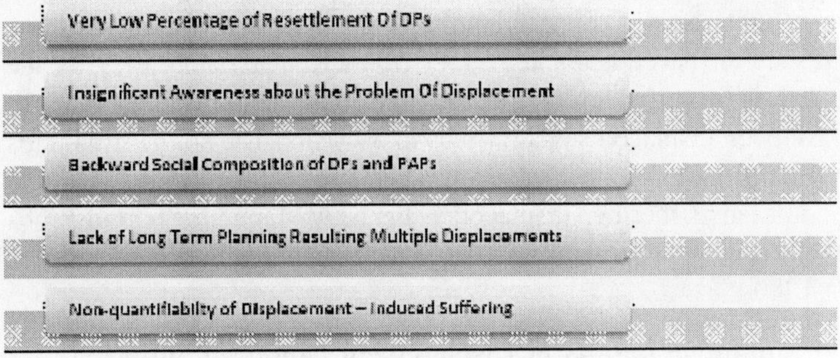

Figure 2.2 Features of Post-independence development

(a) Very Low Percentage of Resettlement of DPs

1/3rd of the DPs have been resettled partially[6]. Three states Madhya Pradesh, Karnataka and Maharashtra have their own State laws. Odisha and Rajasthan have their own polices for the rehabilitation of DPs. National Thermal Power Corporation (NTPC) and coal India promulgated their policies in 1990. Though there is no rehabilitation law prior, the central government came out with a national policy on Resettlement and Rehabilitation for project Affected Families in February 2004 and a draft policy in 2006.

(b) Insignificant Awareness about the Problem of Displacement

Despite the enormity of the problem, awareness level is very low. The number of DPs and PAPs is estimated to be double the 15,000,000 figure, equivalent to which people exchanged borders between India and Pakistan in 1947.

(c) Backward Social Composition of DPs and PAPs

Most of the DPs and PAPs are without any assets and consist of poor rural people like landless labourers, marginal farmers etc. Tribal people are the most affected part due to Displacement. Tribals who are 8.2 per cent of the total population are estimated to be more than 40 per cent of total DPS and PAPs. Dalits are other big victims of displacement. The large portion of the rest belongs to rural background. Most of the DPs and PAPs are rural poor or Dalits or Tribals.

(d) Lack of Long-term Planning Resulting Multiple Displacements

Due to lack of proper planning and proper R & R policies some DPs are displaced again and again. Many Rihand dam oustees of the early 1960s in the border area of Uttar Pradesh and Madhya Pradesh have been displaced several times in 30 years. The soliga tribal DPs again displaced by the displacement because of Rajiv Gandhi National Park. Many fishermen displaced by the New Mangalore port in 1960s and resettled as farmers were displaced again by Konkan Railways in 1980s.

(e) Non-quantifiabilty of Displacement ˘ Induced Suffering

It is very difficult to quantify the suffering of DPs caused by the displacement. Very few DPs from the economically better off groups living in advanced districts may improve their livelihood by getting some compensation for not very fertile and productive land. But most tribal and Dalits and poor rurals who are the main DPs experience financial, social and cultural deterioration. Among all the DPs women pays the highest price for Displacement. The decision makers always plan financial and technical aspects of development projects meticulously. But very little effort is put in getting a clear idea of the living patterns and multiple needs of people affected in planning their resettlement. When resettlement is planned the specificity of the problem faced by the marginalised groups, women and children is ignored. Planners do not very often collect information on the DPs and PAPs which is crucial for minimising displacement, planning rehabilitation and for an accurate cost-benefit analysis. After the introduction of modernisation and globalisation in India, without a change in the unequal social system primarily middle and upper classed were benefitted but poverty has increased it's area and is growing further. The main focus of police makers and private entrepreneurs is on profit. They wanted public sector infrastructure to provide power and raw material and there was little thinking about social components for those who pays everything for the development.

Predominance of Dalits and Tribals among the DPs And PAPs

Various studies confirm that tribals and Dalits have suffered the most. In Odisha the tribals are 22 per cent of the population but comprise 42 per cent of DPs and PAPs. In Andhra Pradesh tribals comprise more than 6 per cent but are 27 per cent of the DPs and PAPs. In Kerala tribals comprise more than 1 per cent of the population but majority among DPs and PAPs are tribals. The story is almost same in Karnataka. Similarly, Dalits are 16 per cent of the population of total India but 20 per cent of DPs and PAPs. Even Other Backward Caste (OBC) people are more in per cent among DPs and PAPs than their per cent of Indian population. So always the weakest section of the society is displaced. The Tribal and Dalit DPs and PAPs are underestimated and are often robbed of their identity. According to "Land Acquisition Act" only patta holders are recognised to get compensation. But a very large number of tribals lack patta. Most tribals traditionally had forests as their sustenance. They don't have the patta of the land on which they depend to earn their livelihood from many years. Similarly, most Dalits are landless labourers, who live by rendering service to the village as a community. Being without a patta both Tribals and Dalits are not counted legally among the DPs and PAPs.

Number of Resettled Person

According to various surveys there as a huge gap between the numbers of people deprived of their livelihood for the sake of development and number of people actually resettled. In Andhra Pradesh little over 26 per cent of the DPs have been resettled partially. In Odisha the resettlement per cent is around 33. In Goa it is about 40 per cent. So in overall not more than 30 per cent to 35 per cent of PDPs have been resettled till now. Even studies show that the quality of resettlement is poor. For example NTPC and Coal India give some jobs to their DPs. Various semi-skilled and skilled jobs are given to those who already possess skills. But many projects which displace people do not prepare them for the new jobs and occupation. Persons from dominant groups usually possess the skills required for the project. Most tribal and Dalit DPs have no access to education and let out without job.

Clauses like the DP should be patta holder, having minimum 2 to 3 acre of land, must be a matriculate very often closes the fate of landless poor. These clauses go against the vulnerable people. Usually only boys from dominant classes reach the higher education or metric level in rural areas. So Tribals, Dalits and mainly women are excluded from the official beneficiary list. A majority of DPs who are poor have little or less contact with the formal sector than other citizen are pushed into a new economy without much preparation. For Ex: a large number of DPs employed by Rourkela steel plant were dismissed for indiscipline, drunken behavior and lack of punctuality. These people were earlier living in an informal agricultural economy and they were unable to cope with new changes. The resettlement and rehabilitation package of development projects are many times nominal relief and are not proper steps towards rehabilitation[7] .

Around 2/3rd of Displaced Persons are not resettled at all. Their situation is worse than that of those who get nominal facilities. For ex the supreme court appointed ombudsmen found that out of around 150000 labourers constructing stadium and other infrastructure for the Asiad Village in New Delhi in 1982, 30 to 40 thousand were slave labourers lured to Delhi by labour contractors with a promise of sending them to Gulf countries. When they were asked why they followed the labour contractor, the labourers told the ombudsmen that they had lost their livelihood to deforestation by industry or due to displacement. The Heavy Electrical Corporation (HEC) at Hatia near Ranchi consumed its capital because of recurring losses. Heavy Electrical Corporation (HEC) has not yet resettled it's DPs who are mostly tribal. Many DPs of HEC are now earning their livelihood by pulling rickshaw in Hatia, Ranchi and nearby towns. Many DPs are working as labourers in brick kiln in Bihar and U.P. Because of their powerlessness many of them loose hope of improving themselves and of attain freedom from this miserable condition. Thus, the weak become totally powerless. To this the extent of Rehabilitation in India can be presented here for reference.

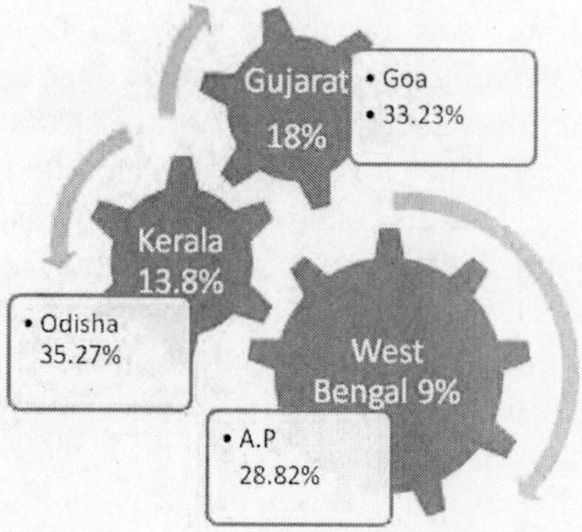

Source: Website

Figure 2.3 : Extent of Rehabilitation

Impact of Globalisation on Displacement

After 1990 Globalisation is a word which reaches even rural people of India. In simple words globalisation refers to the process of integrating the local and national economy with the world economy which is controlled by the rich countries. It involves opening public and private sector industries of India to foreign trade and investment. The logic put towards is that opening up the economy increases economic growth, which in turn results in poverty reduction. But in our country after globalisation the rich become more rich and the poor becomes more poor. Agency like International Monetary Fund and World Bank circulate impressive figures of growth rates, per capita income infrastructure development etc. But the story is quite different for the poor and weaker section of society. Their standard of living is reducing. The process that leads to New Economic Policy 1991 began in 80s when in the face of severe resource crunch, India went for a loan from the IMF. The loan came with a set of conditions that resulted in measure changes in the economic policies. It meant opening up of the economy to the private sector and reduction in Government expenditure in social sector. This was in keeping with the convergence of the interests of global industry and Indian private enterprises. The assumption was to become buoyant the economy should be market led, which required the withdrawal of "license permit Raj" means permission of the Government required to set up industries. The system of "license permit" was introduced in the 1950s to ensure that the private sector should invest in those areas of the economy which is linked with consumer goods and are beneficial to the biggest possible number of citizens. The Government in a hurry to catch up with the rich countries and take the country to the twenty first century adopted the open economy. In the open economic era the Indian Industrialists who have enough influence on political leaders extracted massive concession for themselves and their global allies. The focus shifted to capital intensive technology and export oriented growth. As a result poverty alleviation programmes, employment generation programme are sidelined. For ex in 1987 there are 30 million workers in formal sector. But the number is reduced to 29 million by 1990[8] .

The open economic policy of Government of India of 1980s strengthen after 1991, when under international pressure the Government adopted stabilisation and structural reform measures known as the (New Economic Policy) NEP. The short-term objective of the NEP was to meet the balance of payment crisis, shortage of foreign exchange etc.. In the long run the NEP put the economy on the path of higher growth through increased internal and external investments. NEP resulted in,

(a) Removal of license and permit Raj system.
(b) Deregulation of industrial and financial controls
(c) Removal of subsidies.
(d) Liberalisation of international trade by means of removing export subsidies, reducing import duties, attract foreign capital, use of modern technology etc.

The main effort of New Economic Policy is to remove the few existing hurdles to provide the private sector a free run of the economy and to welcome foreign investors. After NEP foreign capital and multinational companies were offered every facility to use India's raw material and cheap labour. They were also allowed to sell their finished products to one of the fastest growing Indian middle class market. The main target of foreign companies is to acquire the Indian middle class which is more than 250 million. The introduction of a market friendly economy set India on the direct route of industrialisation and development. A growth rate of 6 to 8 per cent that seemed unattainable was achieved soon. But it's benefits goes mainly to monopoly houses and multinationals. In other words the market friendly economy further accentuated the misery of the majority of the population because of rising living costs and higher unemployment.

After NEP the sector composition of GDP growth has not been favourable to poverty reduction especially there is no growth in per capita agricultural production in 1990s than in 80s. The increase of rate of GDP growth is due to a rapid expansion of the service sector. A major increase in regional disparities has been observed during 1990s. Growth rates were relatively high in much of the southern and western regions. On the other hand, there was little growth of per capita income in several of poorer states including Odisha, Bihar, and Uttar Pradesh etc. There were also signs of increasing inequality in the personal distribution of income.

Impact of Displacement

On every creation of God there is some positive and negative effect. Similarly, impact of displacement can be mainly divided into two broad categories. They are:

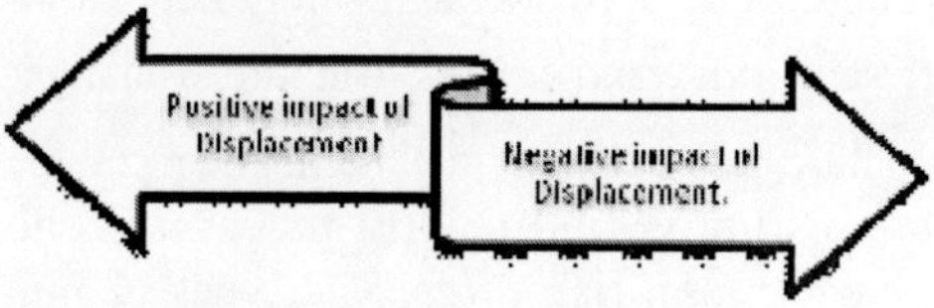

(a) Positive impact of Displacement.

(b) Negative impact of Displacement.

(a) Positive Impact

The positive impacts of displacement however affect only a minuscule section of the affected community. The positive impacts are:

(a) A rise in income may occur in certain cases by the employment opportunities created by the project.

(b) Few persons may experience improvement in their status as they get a bigger amount as compensation for their useless and not so fertile lands.

(c) The economy of the periphery of the project may develop due to the project.

(b) Negative Impact

Majority of the displaced people undergo a process of dispossession. As an outcome of the process of development, displacement has the potential to destroy villages as well as socio-economic and cultural structures of the inhabitants. As displacement in maximum cases a forcible action following are the negative impacts.

(1) Productive asserts and incomes get lost.

(2) People get relocated to environment where there productive skills may be less applicable and the competition for resources is much greater than their original place.

(3) Long established residential groups get disorganised.

(4) Kinship groups get scattered.

(5) Production system gets dismantled.

(6) Informal social networks and safety nets are broken.

(7) Socio-economic and culture structure is changed completely.

Thus by nature displacement in general and forcible displacement particular is a disruptive and painful process. Economically and culturally it creates high risk of chronic types of impoverishment among the displaced people.

Dispossession: Economic Sphere

The dispossession resulting from displacement takes various forms such as economic, social, cultural, political, psychological and environment. They have different impacts on different types of persons involved like small and medium farmers, tribals, landless labours, women and other displaced people. Also there are differences in terms of stresses faced by the various groups.

The economic impacts of displacement on DPs or PAPs are as follows.

(1) Landlessness

Loss of land and change in land holding patterns is one of the principal impacts of displacement. Expropriation of land removes the main foundation upon which people's productive systems, commercial activities and livelihoods are constructed. Due to loss of land people lose their agricultural and homestead land that provides food and economic security to them. If these livelihood systems are not rebuilt elsewhere or replaced with steady income generating employment then landlessness leads to impoverishment. Various types of people, social groups and villages experience the risk of landlessness differently. Balaji Pandey in his study of four villages of Jambubahali, Hensmul, Brahmanbahal and Lakhmanpur in Odisha where large scale displacement resulted from the Talcher mining projects found that in each of these villages the number of landless people had increased after displacement. Some of the variations identified are as follows.

Rise in number of landless – In Bramhanbahal and Jamubahali the number of landless people increased from 20.97 to 90.37 and 36.42 to 84.77 per cent respectively. In these 2 villages most households used to own land before the project came into the area.

Variation in terms of caste group – About 3/4th (73.17 per cent) of the households of the high castes owned the land. However, after displacement only 1/5th (20.49 per cent) of them have their own land. Therefore, in these households, landlessness had risen from 26.83 to 79.51 per cent. However, the increase in the landless category has been highest among the schedule Tribe (58.40) followed by other caste categories (52.68 per cent) and the schedule Castes (42. 60 per cent). There was also a decrease in the number of marginal, small and medium land holding households[9].

(2) Homelessness

Due to displacement many people lose their home. So homelessness is another form of economic dispossession. Though the loss of housing is temporary for most displaced persons this phase can be very long and traumatic by nature. In the early 1970s there is no provision of construction of houses for displaced people by the project authorities. Displaced people were provided with homestead plots on which the DPs were expected to build their own house. For example due to Bokaro steel plant in Jharkhand DPs go through harrowing experiences as a result of homelessness. The ousters of Bokaro Steel Plant were brought from their original place and dumped on an open ground with not even a temporary roof over their heads. The DPs remained in this state of homelessness for 2 to 3 years and had to make do with tents during the period. Due to negligence the project authorities had not made provision for enough homestead plots for all the oustees. Due to which there was a mad rush among the DPs to find a place in the resettlement colony. On the basis of first come first get those who reached the spot first found a plot. The rest were rendered homeless[10].

Due to displacement the people have to leave their own home with which they are acquainted since their birth. But after displacement the displaced people have to live in a new condition. In most of the cases they have to live in poor quality houses. Poor atmospheric conditions make their life more difficult. At some resettlement sites of Sardar Sarovar Dam people used whatever salvaged materials they could carry from their original house to build their new house at resettlement colony or the place where they started to live. Though R & R process supported the dismantling and transportation of the materials some of the building materials were damaged during the transportation as a result of which the new houses are of poor quality. In another example outsets of tentalew and sukka were able to construct only semi-pucca houses which were not suitable for the monsoons in the area. Before submergence their houses were built on hillsides where rain water did not collect because of the natural drainage on the slopes. Now in the new place the DPs complained that they could not afford to construct concrete floors as a result of which the rain water which is collected inside their houses created several problems for them.

(3) Joblessness

Due to displacement DPs undergo a phase when there have no jobs this joblessness is more crucial in case of tribals who depend upon forest for a square meal. So loss of wage employment and shift in the occupational pattern is another form of economic dispossession. It occurs both in urban and rural displacement. Different categories of people are involved in the process of joblessness and occupational shift.

The main convicts are the farmers who are deprived of their farming capacity with loss of land leading to joblessness and resultant impoverishment if not provided with alternate livelihood system. In the village of kunchipadar in Odisha large tracts of land were taken over by the Utkal Auminium India Limited (UAIL) Aluminium Plant. As a result of which both land owner and landless people of the projected area of company lose their livelihood and job. Since no one was losing his or her homestead the company's rehabilitation and resettlement package for jobs to be given to one person per family losing both homestead and land was not applicable to any family of the village. Thus in this village nobody was entitled for a job. As a result of which number of jobless people was very high among the displaced people[11].

In the process of displacement those without asserts and lands are the most vulnerable. This is because neither the state policies nor the Resettlement and Rehabilitation programmes make any clear cut provision for these categories. Many a time they are not considered as the oustees. Even the few jobs that some oustees get in a project after displacement are of temporary in nature for which also they have to pay bribe to some agents. Vocational training of feared to DPs can provide skill but not necessarily jobs. A study of the displacement in the Narmada Project showed that the oustees who were employed by the project authorities were given temporary and lower level posts of peons and the job is contractual in nature. In the meantime the authorities have set up a training institute in village kevadia to provide different vocational skills to the ousters. However, it was found that oustees were not satisfied with the imparting of training only since the training did not assure them a job. So they demanded job in place of skill development[12]. There are employed landless who lose out in the process in 3 ways.

- Loose work on land owned by others, on leased or share cropped land.

- Loose job opportunities primarily in the urban area.
- Loose the use of assets under the common property regime.

An example of this is Mangalore Harbour Project which was commissioned in 1964 in Penambur of Mangalore. In this Project the tenant, cultivators and fish workers were not eligible for any compensation. As a result of which they had to face undue problems in resettling their families. They had to change both their residence and vocation. The eviction however appeared to be a boon to the absentee landlords who fought tooth and nail to get maximum compensation. But the tenant cultivators, agricultural labourers, and other workers of the area neither get any job nor any compensation in terms of money[13].

Displacement also implies occupational shifts and oustees are forced to shift from the type of occupation they were engaged in before displacement. This situation many times creates a situation of underemployment that can be psychologically quite traumatic for the affected people. A survey of the Upper Indrâvati hydro electricity project displacement process brought forth that the number of people engaged in wage labour increased after displacement. Before displacement 4719 persons from 2744 families substituted on wage labour. But after displacement the number rose to 5248 person from 2814 families. Similarly, the number of families engaged in traditional skilled works came down from 67 to 60 after displacement[14].

(4) Loss of Livelihood and Impoverishment

Impoverishment is a process of decline in the economic position of the oustees due to loss of basic sources of livelihood. Landlessness, joblessness, Homelessness are all indicators of the process of marginalisation. It occurs when the family cannot restore it's lost economic strength. It is an indication that the loss of land, productive assets and livelihood have resulted in downward mobility. In this process the middle income farm households don't become landless but become small holders. Families that were earlier just above poverty line fall below it and never recover totally even though they may not become landless. In the case of farming families, partial but significant loss of family land for development work may make some farms economically non-viable. The case of Rihand dam oustees, particularly the tribals, is a case in point of the process of marginalisation. After having lost their land and common property the oustees fell into the typical cycle of increasing debt bondage, coupled with increasing destitution and irregular employment as contract labourers in coalmines and some other places. Many of them are also simply thrown out of job and were left with nothing after some time[15].

The process of impoverishment is often looked at through the perspective of loss of livelihood in general. But it is very necessary to give specific attention to the impoverishment of women. This is mainly because land acquisition and displacement have specific adverse impacts on their status in the family as well as in the community. Women in the tribal areas play an important role in the family's economy based on shifting cultivation, settled agriculture and access to non-timber produce. With displacement and loss of land, women lose the economic autonomy they once enjoyed and become totally subjugated to male domination. Women of Languabeda, Sagadipal, Balangir three of the 5 villages submerged in Rengali Barriage Project at Samal are the example of women's impoverishment. After displacement their land was impounded and they can't get alternative land. Before displacement they use to supervise agricultural operations and retained a part of marketable surplus. They feel that they have been totally subjugated to the men as economic entry. The gender inequalities have been heightened after displacement. Unmarried girls of Sagadipal and Languabeda revealed that the marriage market had suddenly shrunk for them and dowry rates had gone up[16] .

In the process of displacement children are also very vulnerable group. Displacement and relocation often interrupts schooling. Many children even never return to school. After displacement there is a drop in family income. As a result of which many children are draften into the labour market earlier than they would have been. In these conditions girl child are more vulnerable than the male child.

5. Loss of Access to Common Property Resources -

Loss of Common Property Resources (CPRs) results in economic social and cultural dispossession and impoverishment for the oustees, especially the CPR dependants. For poor households in India, particularly the landless and other assetless communities, including women, the Common Property Resources (CPRs) have always been a critical source of livelihood. Fruit and other edible products, firewood and dead wood for use and sale, common grazing areas, medicinal herbs account for a significant share of poor household's resources. Thus the loss of the CPRs results in major income loss or livelihood deterioration particularly for the poor group. CPRs are also of crucial importance for the future of tribal oustees particularly in terms of their indigenous knowledge system may be lost due to disappearing resources, degradation of environment and the loss of those who possess generation's traditional knowledge. The knowledge and skills of the communities need to be conserved not only in their old villages and nearby forests but also in resettlement sites, farms, surrogate forests, water bodies etc.

6. Food Insecurity

Food insecurity is caused by loss of land, livelihood and access to non-timber products. Because of displacement, there is a drop in food production. Displacement also results in loss of harvests. Rebuilding of food production capacity at relocation site may take years. These losses affect food consumption. It results in food insecurity which is defined as intake levels of calories of proteins far below the minimum necessary for the normal growth and work. Food insecurity worsens particularly during the pre-monsoon period when resettlement normally takes place. Displacement also leads to change in dietary intake in the household and that may adversely affect the nutrition level, more specifically of women and children.

The fact has been described in the figure 2.4

Figure 2.4: Dispossession: Economic Sphere

Deficiency: Environmental and Health Spheres

Displacement caused by developmental reasons gives rise to numerous problems in the spheres of environment and health as well. Due to industrialisation deforestation occurs in extensive amount. Due to large scale relocation of DPs to another site sometimes trigger off epidemic and other serious illness.

1. Environmental Impact

Environmental status largely depends upon availability and utilisation of facilities of safe drinking water supply and drainage. Insufficient disposal of solid waste, air and noise pollution etc. may create many environmental hazards which affect the DPs and environment adversely. Due to large industries huge amount of deforestation is done which affect the environment negatively. Many industries use under soil water instead of using water from river as it cost lower to them. As a result of which the under water level in the purifier decreases very fast and put adverse impact on environment. At the plants of NALCO in Odisha emission of pollutants in to the air, release of effluents into water and dumping of solid wastes on open grounds caused many hazards to lives of people, animal and plants of nearby area. A major problem of soil erosion, associated with strip mining and wind erosion has been imposed in the region. The problem becomes acute when the bauxite is dry and rain water erosion is active. Open case mining seems to be generating 25 kg dust per metric tons of bauxite mining during digging, stock filling, loading and dying operation. Air pollution from exhaust fames due to heavy vehicular movements and noise pollution has also increased. All this leads to serious threat to environment and spreading serious disease to crop, people and animals[17].

2. Health Impact

Displacement negatively affects the health status of the community which is a sensitive indicator of development. It has also been seen that people forced to relocate have a higher degree of exposure to illness. Adverse health effects of displacement result particularly when projects don't incorporate preventive epidemiological measures. Preventive health measures rank from diseases of poor hygiene such as diarrhea and dysentery to out brakes of parasitic and vector-borne disease such as malaria and schistosomiasis caused by unsafe, insufficient water supplies and inadequate sanitary waste systems. Studies on displacement have shown that development of large water bodies results on the spread of waterborne diseases, malaria being the prime disease. For ex A crippling bone disease (known as knock-knee) began to appear in the area after the construction of Nagarjuna Sagar dam. A similar bone disease has been reported in the area of Ganganagar through which the Rajasthan canal flows and where many of the pong dam oustees have been resettled.

Dispossession Faced: Social, Cultural, Political and Psychological Spheres

Displacement not only deteriorates a family or a person economically but also socially and psychologically. It takes various forms such as social disorganisation, low self esteem, loss of health, loss of identity, loss of political institution and most important loss of identity culture. All these lead to marginalisation of outstees.

(1) Social Disorganisation

Social disorganisation takes place with the type of changes that are brought about by the displacement process. These forces lead to major changes in the social structure of the communities in general and especially of tribal societies. Their family life may be disrupted. The traditional social control mechanism may be weakened and even lost. Consequently social tension may increase. Also social support network tend to disintegrate and that has far reaching consequences for the community. Social networks often help people cope with poverty through personalised strategies such as informal loans, exchange of food, clothing, durable goods, mutual help with farming building houses and caring for children. Loss of such multifunctional and invisible social networks due to displacement acts as a hidden but serious cause of impoverishment. Such loss is very high in projects that relocate people in a dispersed manner rather than in social groups and units. One example is oustees of Rengali Project in Odisha. After displacement the relationship between the people of the village broke down completely because the families were spread out in different resettlement sites. Therefore, the displaced persons were not properly served by the traditional service caste men. They were relegated to a lower social status. The neighboring villages labeled them as "budiloka" which not only refers to the people of submerged area but also conveys and inferior status. Because of the low estimation of the social status of the oustees by the neighbours, getting brides for the boys has become a problem and getting grooms for their daughter require higher dowry[18].

(2) Loss of Self Esteem and Identity

Often the development project oustees, experience loss of self esteem as individual and as a community. The loss of the moral worth and dignity of a village community can be substantial and as well as socially crippling. Various studies have shown that tribals, who have strong community ties and have yet to get into the mainstream market economy, feel threatened by Government power hierarchy. After relocation they are further fragmented, weakened and inherently unable to organise themselves. The disappearing community ties caused by geographical dispersal and the threat of commercial forces squeeze their spirits further[19].

(3) Loss of Culture and Religion

Due to displacement the oustees also face the risk of losing their culture and religious practices. They loose their cultural autonomy and in the process, their very identity is put at stake. Consequently every area of their life from language to marriage customs religion comes under attack. There is a gradual collapse of the religious ethos that is closely linked to their environment and socio-agrarian system. The community festivals, which held tremendous importance in the lives of the people, lose their meaning.

(4) Loss of Political Institutions

In the political sphere dispossession takes place through the process of political integration in the so called national polity. This gradually leads to the traditional political system's redundancy. The DPs are incorporated into the state and have to confirm to and become integrated with the so called mainstream political system.

(5) Psychological Impact

Displacement and dislocation causes special cultural, economic and technical problems. Studies have shown that a feeling of alienation, helplessness and powerlessness is instilled in those uprooted. Social cohesion is weakened and increased psychological stress diminishes the initiative and capacity for collective action of those affected. Displacement may also lead to social anomie and emotional disorders. Many indicators of social anomie such as alcoholism, crime, suicides, prostitution, delinquency and despair may go up[20] .

The figure 2.5 explains the above facts

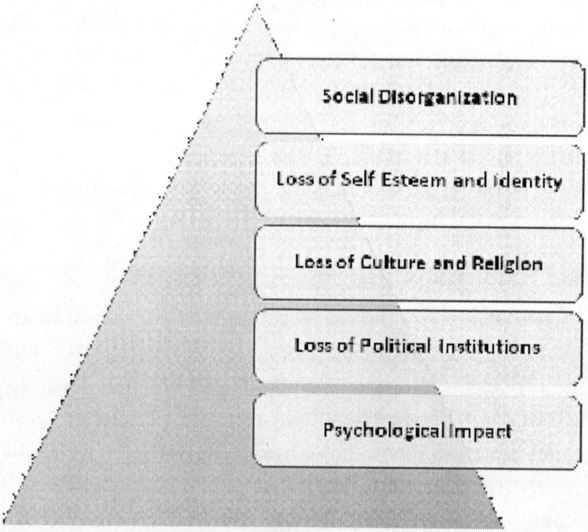

Figure 2.5 : Impacts Displacement

Legal Aspects of Displacement

People are displaced mostly because their lands and homes are acquired. Sometimes their common resources are also taken away. As per the legal point of view there are certain rules for acquiring land. These rules provide us with the operating context within which displacement occurs. The Land Acquisition Act, 1894 is the mother act of all acts regarding displacement and land acquisition. There are also different acts like the National Highways Act. The Coal Bearing Areas Act that allows the Government to acquire land for the specific purpose of the act. These acts lay down the rules the Government must follow before the Government can take away any one's land. But the Government must give the people notice and the Government must tell them why it wants their land. People are allowed to challenge the Government. The Government must pay them for their land and other benefits. There are rules for calculating the cost of the land as well as for making the payments. If those rules are not followed then court can make the Government return the land.

Prior to 1944 LAA 1894 was not applicable to the states of Jammu and Kashmir, Rajasthan, Kerala and Nagaland which had their self contained Land Acquisition Acts. In 1984 LAA (Amendment) Act was passed. The extent of its applicability was extended to the whole India except Jammu and Kashmir which enjoys a special position under the construction and still continues to be governed by the State (J & K) Land Acquisition Act, 1990. The Land Acquisition Act, 1894 was amended in 1984 by the central Government to remove various bottlenecks of the original Act and increasing its applicable efficiency.

Since independence, the country has witnessed an accelerated case of economic development. There has been a tremendous spurt in the number of development projects taken up by the State. Industries, dams, mines, thermal power plants, highways, Railways etc. require vast quantities of land. Since majority of the people live in rural area and depend on land for their livelihood, there is hardly any land that is not used or occupied. So the land has to be acquired or taken away from the existing occupants and users which will cause displacement. It is known that the state has the right to command and appropriate for itself, lands situated within it's jurisdiction provided it is for purposes of some public utility. The State has the power to taken property for public use without owner's consent. This is known as the right of eminent domain of the State. The right of eminent domain is the basis of Land Acquisition Act, 1894 which is directly and exclusively concerned with the acquisition of land by the central as well as the State Government.

Power of State Government to Amend the Land Acquisition Act, 1984.

The Land Acquisition Act 1984 has been enacted by the Central Government. However, the State Government has the power to amend its provisions. Within the territory of each State, the Act will be applicable in the amended form. The State Government can make any amendments as long as they are not opposed to any of the provisions of the Act.

Features of Land Acquisition (Amended) Act, 1984.

The Land Acquisition Act, 1894 was drastically amended in 1964 by the Central Government Following are some features of Land Acquisition Act, 1984.

- The setting down of a time limit for the completion of all formalities between the issue of the preliminary notice under section 4(1) of the act and the issue of declaration of intended acquisition under section 6(1) of the Act, [First provision to section 6(1) of LA Act].
- The setting down of a time limit within which the collector must make his/her award (section II-A of the Act).
- Payment of interest at 12 per cent per annum for the period commencing from the date of the notice under section 4(1) of L A Act and ending with the date of the collector's award. [Section 23 (I-A) of LA Act].
- Payment of solatium (i. e. compensation for loss, suffering or injured feelings) at an increased rate of 30 per cent of the market value of the acquired land (section 23(2) of LAA). Previously the interest rate was fixed at 15 per cent of the market value.
- The provision of an opportunity to those dissatisfied with the collector's award to apply to him/her for a redetermination of the compensation payable to them on the basis of an order for higher compensation obtained by any one of them from the Reference Court (Section 28 – A of L A Act).

These important changes made by the amendment are very beneficial for the displaced person because due to these changes the undue delays which characterise acquisition proceedings are minimised. These changes also provide for payment of compensation on a realistic scale.

Acquisition of Land for Companies

Under the provision of LAA 1984 land can be acquired for a public purpose and for a company. Same procedures are to be followed to acquire land for a company as well as public purpose. But no steps can be taken to acquire land for a company unless.

- Consent of Government has been obtained.
- The company has executed agreements written below (Section 39 of the Act).
- For the purpose of this Act the term "company" includes following.
- Companies in the strict sense of the term as defined in the Companies Act, 1956.
- Societies registered under societies Registration Act, 1860.
- Cooperative societies within the meaning of any State laws pertaining to co-operative societies [section 3(a) of the Act]
- Industrial concerns owned by an individual or an association of individuals (Partnership firm employing at least 100 workers). – land can be acquired for such a concern if it is needed for two purposes namely-
- Erecting dwelling houses (residences) for workmen employed by it.
- Providing amenities directly connected with the above purpose e.g. sewage, sanitation.

The preliminary notice under section 4(1) of the act can be issued by the Government before these 2 conditions have been complied with but the Government may not issue the declaration under Section 6 of Land Acquisition Act until these conditions have been fulfilled. After the amendment Act of 1984 acquisition of land for a corporation owned or controlled by the State (For ex the FC/or the State Trading Corporation etc.) is automatically regarded as a public purpose.

Consent of Government

When a company makes an application to the Government for acquiring any land the Government directs the collector or an authorised officer to submit a report on whole matter. The report generally consists following areas—

(a) Whether the company has made all reasonable efforts to get the land in question by negotiation with the owners of such land offering to pay a reasonable price and that such efforts have failed.

(b) Whether the land in question is suitable for the purpose for which it is to be acquired.

(c) Whether the company is in a position to utilise the land speedily and efficiently.

Purpose of Acquisition ˇ Section 40(1) of the Act

The Government must also be satisfied that the company requires the land for one of the following purposes—

- To obtain land for erecting dwelling houses for workmen employed by it or for the provision of amenities directly connected therewith eg. Sanitation, sewage [Section 40(1) (a) of the Act].
- For the construction of some building on work for a company which is engaged or is taking steps for engaging itself in any industry or work, which is for public purposes. [Section. 40(1) of the Act.]
- For the construction of some work andthat such work is likely to prove useful to the public [Section 40(1)(b) of Act] A hospital, a public reading room or an educational institution open to the public would fall on this category.

Agreement with the Government Section 41 of the Act

Once the Government is satisfied that the company desires to acquire land for a purpose which is sanctioned by the Act and also fulfills the other conditions prescribed in rule 4 of the LA (Companies)

Rules 1963, then, it can require the company to enter into an agreement with it providing for the following matters such as—

- The payment to the Government of the cost of acquisition no declaration under section 6 of the act can be issued unless the entire compensation amount will be paid by such company.
- The terms on which the land will be held by the company (Section. 44-A of the LAA) prohibits any company for which land has been acquired from transferring the same without the previous sanction of the collector. The provision is intended to prevent misuse of acquire land.

Publication of Agreement- Section 42 of Act

Once the agreement has been executed it must be published in the official Gazette just like a Section 4(1) of the Act notification. There after the declaration under Section 6 of the act will be made and the rest of the procedure laid down in the Act will follow.

Limitations of the Land Acquisition Act

The Land Acquisition Act as amended does not contain any provision specifically dealing with resettlement (including that related to income restoration aspects).

- It does not allow for compensation (except for houses) for landless laborers, artisans, and those sharing the use of land but without legal rights to it;
- The method of valuation of land considers only the market price of land at the date of notification under Section 4(1) but ignores any increase in the value of land at a subsequent date. Compensating for actual market value of land, which will entitle the owner to buy similar replacement land in adjacent areas, is not practicable under the framework of the Land Acquisition Act;
- The Act computes the value of land through the sales statistics method, leading to undervaluation of land. Buyers deliberately undervalue their land in sales transactions to reduce registration fees. This leads to a large number of court cases resulting in further delays and harassment both to landowners and the LAO/project authority (PA);

- The Act does not specify any compensation for deprivation of CPRs, especially loss of customary rights to land and forests, which forms an integral part of tribal livelihoods;
- The acquisition process takes too long and is incompatible with infrastructure project construction schedules.

Other Acts for Land Acquisition

Land Acquisition Act. 1894 is the basic Act. under which land is acquired for public purpose. There are also some other Acts. under which land can be acquired for a specific purpose. Some of these Acts are

- The National Highways Act 1956;
- Coal Bearing Areas (Acquisition and Development) Act, 1957;
- Maneuvers field firing and Artillery Practice Act, 1938.

National Highways Act 1956 (NHA)

National Highways are the life line of India. National Highways are very important for transport and communication. They pass through more than one State. The National Highways Act was passed in order to put development and maintenance of National Highways under one authority. The authority is the NHAI (National Highways Authority of India). This Act was passed in 1956 and came to effect from 15th April 1957. The NHA was amended in 1977, with these amendments the NHA has changed a lot and is different now from its original form and content. Under section 2 of the NHA the Central Government has the power to declare a highway as NH. It has also the power to declare that a NH shall no longer be NH. In that case that highway will not come under NHA. At the end of the Act there is a list or schedule which contains the details of National Highway. Each NH has a name and a number. For ex- Grand Trunk Road is NH1 and famous Agra- Mumbai road is NH-3(Old NH number). The NHA 1956 is designed to allow the Central Government to acquire land and do everything that has to be done to have an efficient Highways system. It was enacted because it was necessary to keep the development and management of Highways under one authority.

The original Act was amended various times. As a result the original Act has been changed in two fundamental ways. Firstly, the Government is allowed to levy fees, first for ferries and then even for using parts of highways. This means the Government has the right to charge a fee to use the highways. Secondly, the Government was given the power to enter into a contract with private parties to construct the highways, maintain them, collect and keep the fees to recover the cost of construction as well as the cost of maintenance. They can even regulate the traffic within limits of motor vehicle Act. Thirdly, a new offence has been created to punish anyone who damages National Highways.

Difference between Land Acquisition Act and National Highways Act

The Land Acquisition Act & National Highways Act is different as to the regulations. Land is acquired only for National Highways under National Highways Act. Purpose of Land Acquisition Act is solely to regulate land acquisition but the main purpose of NHA is to regulate National Highways. The central Government may issue a notification in the official Gazette and designate any person or authority as a competent authority and give them power to perform specific functions under the Act. There is no competent authority under the Land Acquisition Act. The work of acquiring land is done by collector. The definition of land is same as in Land Acquisition Act.

Coal Bearing Areas (Acquisition and Development) Act, 1957

The CBAA was passed in 1957. Until CBAA was enacted in 1957 land for coal mining was acquired under Land Acquisition Act. This Act applies only to Central Government and only the Central Government can use it to acquire coal bearing land. This Act can only be used for coal bearing areas. It can't be used to acquire land containing any other mineral like iron or copper. The most important distinction of CBAA is that it has special provisions on the rights of license holders and lease holders called lessees. CBAA allows for acquisition of land belonging to a State Government.

The CBAA was enacted to make it possible to centralise the management of coal mining. It allows land belonging to the State Government to vest in the Central Government .This Act lays down rules for dealing with the license holders and lessees. This Act is very harsh on the person who have and interest in the land. Notifications or declarations under this Act are not easily accessible to the ordinary citizen. Compensation is more in the nature of reimbursement. This Act makes it possible for the Government to hand over the management of coal mining to a Government company. Like the NHA this act centralises mining and then hands it over to another.

Manoeuvres Field Firing and Artillery Practice (MFFAP) 1938

MFFAP is a bit different from the above two Acts where Displacement occurs permanently. MFFAP deals only with temporary possession of land hence temporary displacement occurs. The armed forces consist of the Army, the Navy and the Air Force. The Armed forces have to be ready to save the country from any external attack. The armed forces have to defend the borders in case the country is attacked. So they have to test their weapons and carry out mock battles and other trainings. The Navy conducts it's exercise and test the weapons on the sea. The Air Force does it in the Air. Neither Navy nor Air Force needs any land for the testing purpose. But the Army needs land to test it's strength. The Army has to hold its training exercises in a variety of terrain such as desert, Forest, mountain, Flat land etc. so it has to shift the location a number of times. It does not need any land permanently just for the purpose. It only needs to be able to use the land from time to time. This Act is not meant to acquire land. It is intended to allow the Army to use land for its exercises and to test its weapons. The notices under this Act are really meant to reach the people. This is the only Act in which the authority that does damage is required to repair the damage. However, while no area may be notified more than once in 3 years, the Act does not say for how long the area may remain notified. It is legally possible to shift boundaries of the area just by a few feet and it will actually remain under notification for long years.

Forest and Environment Protection Act

More or less every modern country has passed laws to prevent wholesale encroachment by human beings on the habitat of other creatures. These laws earmark land for conservation of nature. Conservation is necessary for our own well being. We need forests for our own well being. As a result of growing deforestation the nature is in danger. We are not above the nature and a part of cycle conducted by nature. If we will try to break the cycle we have to face the ill effect of it. For Ex. China conducted a campaign against birds because the Government thought they ate too much of crops. But birds also used to ate the insects that destroyed the crops. After the Birds were killed the number of insects were multiply unchecked and did tremendous damage to crops. The destruction of forest cover has more alarming effects. Rainfall decreases alarmingly. Rain water is washed away into rivers and disappears into the sea. The soil is washed away and there are landslides. The level of ground water is decreasing rapidly. Due to heavy industrialisation the atmosphere is polluted. All types of climate changes are occurring which are harmful to mankind. Everyday scientists are warning the society about various dangers. So we need to conserve forests and wild life for our own shake. For this purpose India has made several laws to shave its forest. Some of these important Acts are-

- The Wildlife (Protection) Act, 1972
- The Indian Forest Act, 1927
- The Indian Forest (Conservation) Act, 1980

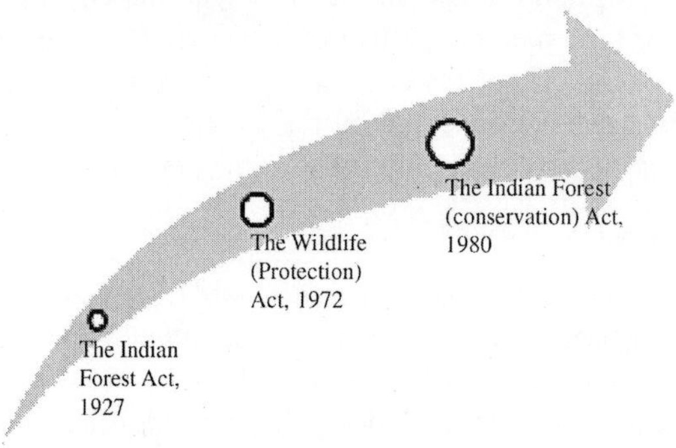

The Wildlife (Protection) Act, 1972

The Wildlife Protection Act aims at protecting all living creatures (not domestic) wherever they may live-on land, in water or in the sky. This includes regulation of zoos and regulation or prohibition of hunting wild animals. Under this act vegetation is also protected. So this act regulates trade in or removal of protected plants or species. There was a time when our land is covered with deep forests. But now-a-day due to heavy industrialisation and population explosion there is a growing demands for land. Forests are cut down for different purposes. As a result wild animals often enter villages or attack cattle or other domestic animals. They even attack human beings. Clearly people need to be protected from wild animals. They have the right to live safely. But the animals also have the right to live safely. One solution of this problem is to reserve a separate space for animals by declaring it to be a sanctuary or a reserve park. But this means denying people the right to use that land or restricting their right to use it.

Difference between LAA and WPA

Wildlife is not a usual Land Acquisition Act. Under LAA the government publishes a notification which says Government wants the land for a public purpose. After a long process the Government publishes a declaration that the land has been acquired. But in case of wildlife Act the government declares it's intention to make a certain area as a sanctuary. A sanctuary is a safe place for wild animals. A sanctuary is a place where the animals may be safe, where they need not fear hunters or other attacks on their life. This act prescribes the powers of two authorities. The land is acquired by collector for a sanctuary or for a national park but it is managed by Chief Wild Life Warden. The Government in this Act is generally the state government. If the territory is administered by the Central, government then the government means the administrator of the territory.

Indian Forest Act, 1927

Indian Forest Act was 1st passed in 1878 and then replaced in 1927. It has been amended several times after Independence. This Act doesn't apply to all of India. After 1956 the Act is applied to the states of Bihar, Bombay, Madhya Pradesh, Odisha, Punjab, Uttar Pradesh and West Bengal. Under this Act the states were given the power to make the Act applicable in part or full to themselves. This Act doesn't define a forest. Nagpur High Court has said that forest may be defined as per the Oxford English Dictionary. A forest is a large track of land covered with trees and other vegetation. It may also have patches of cultivated land. This Act deals with reserved forests and protected forests. Neither of this term is defined in this Act. Under this Act the State Government must issue a notification under Section 4 of the Act. In the official gazette that is intends to constitute any land as a reserved forest. It must specify the limits of the land clearly. It is enough if the notification mentions the rivers, hills or other land marks on the boundaries. It must appoint a forest settlement officer to look into the rights of people.

The Forest Conservation Act, 1980

Forest Conservation Act, 1980 has a sole purpose to conserve forest or to prevent deforestation. The controlling authority is the Central Government. The Act has only four sections. During late 1970s the Government of India was seriously alarmed at the rapidity with which forests were disappearing. Apart from encroachment the State Government themselves were misusing their power under Section 27 of the Forest Act to deserve a reserved forest or to convert any forest land to non-forest uses.

The central government had therefore issued an ordinance in 1980 to control deforestation. Section 2 of the Forest Conservation Act expressly forbids such Acts without prior permission of the central government. The explanation to the section says that clearing the land for coffee, tea, rubber or spice plantation or for growing medicinal plants is putting the land to non-forest use. However, the land may be used to establish check posts, fences, bridges, dams and waterholes etc. that are necessary for management of wild life or forests. For example when Maharashtra Government wanted to give forest lands to settle the Project Affected Persons of Sardar Sarovar Dam the prior permission of the central government had to be taken.

Resettlement and Rehabilitation Policy

After 1947 India saw the rapid onset of planned development which was made possible by the implementation of five year plans. A number of dams power plants, industries, roads were constructed which required acquisition of land. This led to major disruption in land. Hence, the need was felt not only for adequate and equitable laws/policies for land acquisition but also sensitive and effective laws/ policies related to resettlement and rehabilitation.

There are three types of policies for R&R existing in our country:

(a) The first one is sectoral, referring to specific areas of operation like water resources. Two public sector companies have their own policies;

(b) The State R&R Policy. Only two States have got R & R Policy; and

(c) Finally, there is a National Policy on Resettlement and Rehabilitation (NPRR) for project affected families, 2004.

Many social activities and Organisations working for DP/PAPs believe that some sections of these policies are acceptable. But some sections of these are completely unacceptable. As a result of which there is a lack of national consciousness about it in India as a whole. Generally, there are two types of views on the issue of development: First group views development as Gross National Product (GNP) and for that purpose displacement is unfortunate but inevitable; The Second group gives priority to human growth state and says that displacement can be minimised and alternatives are available but the political will to search for them is lacking.

Many people consider compensation a substitute to it. The LAA 1894 under which land is acquired provides for compensation of 'Patta' land alone. Most of the tribals and dalits have no "Patta" of their land. As a result they are big loosers. Different studies have shown that the compensation given is inadequate even for the patta owners. The LAA 1894 allows the state to displace people without their consent in the name of public purpose, which has not been defined even a century after the enactment of LAA. Compensation is based on the market value not on the replacement of the livelihood lost to the project. These are some serious drawbacks of LAA 1894. As a result of this there is a need of an alternate model by which the displacement could have less amount of negative effect.

Various social activities and organisations working for the DPs/ PAPs advocate for policies that move away from the exploitative nature of current policies. They demand that the displacement should always occur with the consent of displaced people. They want the affected communities to be involved in the identification of the assets to be acquired of persons to be displaced, norms for compensation and implementation of the rehabilitation plan. They want a solution should be found to the process that impoverish and marginalise the already weak people.

Due to displacement many people are deprived of their livelihood which results in economic impoverishment as well as social marginalisation. So while calculating profit and losses of the development project one can't stick to the economic definition of impoverishment. One has to definitely consider the cultural, psychological and social issues. So while planning a project the planner has to remember the following observations:

(a) Most DPs/PAPs belong to the semi-monetised informal economy. Some of them sustain themselves on the CPRs and other by rendering service to the village as a community;

(b) Even when their monetary income rises, they are often impoverished in economic terms too because their livelihood for the CPRs is not replaced.

Impoverishment and Marginalisation

Impoverishment is economic. Marginalisation means deterioration in the social status and psychological attitudes of an individual or a community. So marginalisation goes beyond the loss of material resources. It deprives the individual; community to improve their socio-economy status. When the DP/PAP which belong to informal economy pushed into an encounter with the powerful formal sector and the external world without adequate preparation these impoverished communities are often forced to internalise the value system of the new society that does not recognise their own economy and culture. Thus, they develop a sense of helplessness and powerlessness. Such a negative internalisation makes it impossible for them to rebuild their lives. As a result their material and social status as well as psychological attitudes deteriorate and they loose the possibility of beginning a new and improved life.

So to measure the impact of displacement and deprival we have to go beyond economic aspects to cultural, social, psychological and health parameters. One has thus to include components of informal economy such as the CPRs and none economic ones like social disintegration, dispossession and its impact on their health. In R&R policies there are distinction between resettlement and rehabilitation. This distinction is essential because a major cause of impoverishment and marginalisation is the failure to rehabilitate the people even when they are resettled.

Resettlement and Rehabilitation

Resettlement means one time relocation with or without other support such as jobs or the training to deal with new society and economy. Rehabilitation on the other hand means rebuilding the lost livelihood of the DPs/PAPs. It goes beyond economic components to deal with the cultural, social, psychological and the factors that marginalise them. In economic issues it doesn't stop at marketable commodities that the formal economy takes into consideration but also includes the CPRs and other assets of the informal or semi-monetised economy on which most DPs and PAPs depend. Rehabilitation includes non economic components like social disintegration, health issues, the environment and dispossession. The first non-economic factor to be attended to is the trauma of being displaced or deprived without one's consent. The process of marginalisation begins with its profound psychological impact on the DPs/ PAPs. Secondly, they have to be prepared culturally, socially and psychologically to deal with the formal and fully monetised economy they are push into. Lack of that preparation can marginalise them. Giving only monetary compensation or a job without such a preparation can go against their economic as well as social interests. Many industries offer self-employment by way of economic rehabilitation. In some cases monetary compensation alone is given. They cannot be successful without cultural, social and psychological preparation to deal with the inputs. For ex. Tribals displaced by the Hirakud Dam in Odisha in 1950s were not used to monetary economy. They were paid only monetary compensation for the little land they owned. Certain merchants approached them with fake trinkets that looked like gold and luxury items. The tribals did not know the value of the money they got or of the trinkets they bought which were cheap items. In the end they were left with no money but only with fake trinkets. They thus fell into the hands of moneylenders for meeting their basic needs. So rehabilitation has to counteract the process leading to the DPs losing confidence in themselves as individual and giving up any hope of improving themselves.

The National Policy on R&R for Project Affected Families, 2004

Government of India has adopted a National Policy on Resettlement and Rehabilitation (NPRR) from Project Affected Families in 2004 after putting in two decades of preparation phase. Prior to the NPRR, the problems and issues of project affected communities were largely dealt with under the Land Acquisition Act, which primarily dealt with acquisition of land and only provided for compensation for land to the title owners.

When the SC and ST Commission indicated that about 40 per cent of the DPs/ PAPs may be tribals, in 1985 the Ministry of Welfare, appointed a committee under the chairmanship of the SC and ST Commissioner, Dr B. D. Sharma, to prepare a rehabilitation policy for the tribal DPs. The Committee suggested a national policy covering all the DPs, not merely tribal's. It added that rehabilitation should be integral to every project above a certain size in the public as well as private sectors, that it be binding on the Government and the implementing authority and that the policy should have legal authority.

After eight years of the suggestion of B.D. Sharma commission, the Ministry of Rural Development formulated a draft in 1993 and revised it in 1994. The former was drafted by the bureaucrats within the Ministry of Rural Development. The latter was redrafted after getting the reaction of 15 Ministries and Departments. The 1994 draft however, had no such compulsions. It omitted all references to the past and showed no sense of guilt at the suffering of the people. It also does not make any reference to the T.N. Singh formula, which stated that public sector mines and industries give a job to each family that they displaced. The 1994 draft's sole concern remains in 1991 economic policy which begins by stating: With the new economic policy, it is expected that there will be large scale investments...

thereby creating an enhanced demand for land to be provided within a shorter time-span in an increasingly competitive market ruled economic structure. With the opening up of the economy, it is expected that the tribal regions are likely to attract further investments in the near future thereby adding to the demand for land.

Both the 1993 & 1994 drafts saw the need for R&R but did not refer to rehabilitation as a right of the affected people. Though most studies show that women are the worst victims, neither of the drafts made any special provision for them. Both the drafts stressed on allotment of separate sites to major sons but did not mention such provisions for daughters. In 1994-95 more than 1,500 social activist groups joined hands with thousands of DPs/ PAPs. They prepare an alternative policy and presented it to Secretary, Rural Development, Ministry, Govt of India in October 1995. During this period, they first identified the principles on which the R&R policy should be based. The alternative policy suggested having a definite tribal/dalit/ gender bias and ensuring that their special needs are met and the marginalisation prevented. Equal justice to all the DPs/PAPs was stressed upon to be the norm. It suggested that no project that irreversibly disrupts the culture of a community should be permitted. Rehabilitation was stressed on as a right of the DPs.

Features of National Policy On R&R For Project Affected Families, 2004

A final decision on the draft national policy was taken by the GbI only in 2004 and a National Rehabilitation Policy was promulgated on 17 February 2004. The NPRR is applicable to Projects displacing 500 families or more enmasse in plain areas and 250 families' in hilly areas, Desert Development Programme (DDP) blocks, areas mentioned in Schedule V and Schedule VI of the Constitution of India.

The key policy objectives are to:

- Minimise displacement as far as possible by looking for alternatives;
- To Plan R&R of the PAPs taking into account the special needs of the vulnerable groups namely tribal, poor, women, small and marginal farmers etc;

- To Provide better standards of living to the project affected families (PAFs);
- To build a dialogue and a harmonious relationship between the PAFs and the requiring body (Project Authorities).

Benefits of the Policy

Chapter VI of the NPRR lays down comprehensive R&R benefits for the PAFs for various types of losses. The policy recognises various types of losses and provides R&R benefits as below:

- In case of loss of Residential structure, policy provides for free of cost house site; (Para 6.2)
- In case of loss of Agricultural land or cultivable waste land, allotment of agricultural land or cultivable waste land subject to availability of government land; (Para 6.4)
- Provision of land development assistance, in case of allotment of wasteland/degraded land in lieu of acquired land to the PAFs; (Para 6.7)
- Financial assistance to PAF's having cattle for cattle shed construction; (Para 6.8)
- Transportation cost for shifting to PAFs; (Para 6.9)
- Financial assistance to PAF comprising of rural artisan/ small trader and self-employed person; (Para 6.10)
- Financial assistance for agricultural and non-agricultural labour; (Para 6.14)
- Income restoration benefits in the form of necessary training facilities for entrepreneurship development to PAFs; (Para 6.18)
- A separate set of R&R benefits with special assistance to PAFs of Scheduled tribes; (Para 6.21)
- Additional assistance to BPL PAFs;
- Provisions for basic amenities and infrastructural facilities at the Resettlement zones and sites. (Para 6.22)

Despite being an apparent right step forward, the NPRR has been criticised by many. Mainly it does not have any of the progressive clauses that were put in the earlier drafts after consultation with the civil society during 1998-99. It is ironic that the policy recognises the limitations of compensation through cash and states that the system of extending cash compensation does not by itself, in most cases enable the affected families to obtain cultivable agricultural land, homestead and other resources which they have to surrender to the State. However, all that the policy gives to those displaced is some extra cash, but no support for livelihoods.

Draft National Policy, 2006

The Draft National Rehabilitation Policy (NRP) was recently introduced for addressing the enormous issue of Resettlement & Rehabilitation (R&R) of affected populations due to infrastructure development projects. It is an attempt to better address the subject of development induced displacement & to eliminate and integrate certain crucial aspects which were unaddressed in the earlier policy. It reflects certain deviations in National Policy for Resettlement & Rehabilitation, 2004. The whole approach of NRP has a paradigm shift from exclusive welfare based approach to Rights-based approach and has distinct developmental connotations.

Objectives of the Draft Policy

The main objectives of the draft policy are as below:

- The policy acknowledges the fact that displacement causes severe traumatic, psychological and socio-cultural consequences on the displaced populations and thus concerted efforts to uphold their rights is quintessential. The intent lays in minimising displacement as far as possible.
- It reflects the ethos of participatory & consultative approach when it mentions-"there is imperative need to recognise R&R issue as intrinsic to the development process formulated with the active. Participation of affected persons, rather than as externally imposed requirements".
- It has a welcome shift of identifying the affected populations as key stakeholders in the planning stage till the implementation stage.
- Introduction of the mechanism of Tribal Development Plan is a significant incorporation in the R&R plan provision.

- Setting basic minimum provisions for compensation which can be further added upon as per individual project undertakings, however maintaining & ensuring the non-negotiable nature of the provision is a reflection of the equitability of the policy regarding the compensatory measures for the affected population.
- The main objective of this policy is also to promote non-displacing or least displacing alternatives. There is sharp paradigm shift in treatment of the issue. It is best practices promoting endeavour as against its earlier policy (NPRR 2004) in sensitivity of treating displacement as a natural and normal consequence of any kind of infrastructure and other projects.

Features

The Draft NRP is applicable to new projects or expansion project, which involve displacing 400 or more families enmasse in plain areas and 200 families' enmasse in hilly areas, Desert Development Programme (DDP) blocks, and areas mentioned in Schedule V and Schedule VI of the Constitution of India. It acknowledges the component of non-monetary compensations in resettlement & rehabilitation of displaced persons. The principles of the policy can be applied to cases of displacement wherever individuals are affected, however, it is not binding though can be utilised as reference point "the principles of this policy may apply to the rehabilitation of persons displaced due to any reason". Integration of Social Impact Assessment as a tool to measure the desirability and justifiability of the project is a crucial aspects. This will reflect the perceptions of the displaced community regarding the project along with providing a blue print of the extent of losses incurred by them, based upon which the mitigation measures will be applicable to the affected population.

Benefits of NRP

Various important benefits of the draft NRP are as below:

- In case of loss of Residential structure, the policy provides free of cost house site to the extent of actual loss. An additional entitlement is also applicable to a nuclear family; (Para 7.2).

- In case of loss of Agricultural land or cultivable waste land, allotment of agricultural land or cultivable waste land will be provided, subject to availability of government land; it is available to farmers who will turn as marginal farmers as a consequence of the project; (Para 7.4)
- Provision of land development assistance, in case of allotment of wasteland/degraded land in lieu of acquired land to the AFs will be provided; (Para 7.7)
- Financial assistance to AF's having cattle for constructing cattle shed will be provided; (Para 7.8)
- Transportation cost on actual costs basis will be provided for shifting of materials of the AF's; (Para 7.9)
- Financial assistance to AF's comprising of rural artisan/ small trader and self-employed person; (Para 7.10)
- In case of projects involving land acquisition the provision of providing employment to affected persons is available, subject to certain criterions; (Para 7.11)
- Income restoration benefits in the form of necessary training facilities for entrepreneurship development to PAFs; (Para 7.16)
- Separate assistance to SC/ST's will be provided. Assistance for SC's have been included for special assistance for the first time; (Para 7.18)
- Infrastructure facilities and basic amenities will be provided at resettlement zones; (Para 7.19)
- The Policy provides for the formation of a R&R committee at the project label to monitor and review the progress of R&R implementation.

The draft policy has incorporated various developmental parameters however owing to a lack of detailed description of the same a vague depiction is reflected. An extreme fallacy in the policy lays in the provision of establishing the entitlement of affected persons on the parameter of living or using the affected structure/plot for 3 years or more for all affected persons. This condition poses a grave plight to the cause of holistic resettlement & rehabilitation because an affected person should be considered anyone living/using the affected site prior to notification of the project. Another significant limitation lays in the very nature of the policy as it remains a set of guidelines on development induced displacement and lacks legal framework. The provision of employment to affected persons is subject to certain conditions which may act against the livelihood restoration aspect of resettlement and rehabilitation.

Right to Fair Compensation, Resettlement, Rehabilitation and Transparency in Land Acquisition Bill 2013, The Land Acquisition, Rehabilitation and Resettlement Bill - 2011

The Land Acquisition, Rehabilitation and Resettlement Bill -2011 is a historic bill with important implications. This most awaited bill is intended to provide fair compensation and assurance to those whose land is taken away for development and other projects. It aims bringing transparency to the process of acquisition of land to set up factories or buildings and assures rehabilitation. This problem was effectively sorted by industries and those who live off the land. The Act was passed on 29 August 2013 in the Lok Sabha (lower house of the Indian parliament) and on 4 September 2013 in Rajya Sabha (upper house of the Indian Parliament). The bill received the assent of the President of India, Sh. Pranab Mukherjee on 27 September 2013. The Act came into force from 1 January 2014.

The bill aims to replace a nearly 120-year-old law enacted during British rule in 1894. LARR Bill 2011 and LARR 2011 are the other names of The Land Acquisition, Rehabilitation and Resettlement, 2011 Bill. It has 107 clauses. It is the useful regulation for land acquisition as a part of India's massive industrialisation drive fuelled by public-private partnership. The then UPA Government has renamed LARR Bill, 2011 as "Right to Fair Compensation, Resettlement, Rehabilitation and Transparency in Land Acquisition Bill 2013".

Scope of the Act

The Act aims to establish the law on land acquisition, as well as the rehabilitation and resettlement of those directly affected by the land acquisition in India. The scope of the Act includes all land acquisition whether it is done by the Central Government of India, or any State Government of India, except the state of Jammu & Kashmir.

The Act is applicable when:

- Government acquires land for its own use, hold and control, including land for Public sector undertakings.
- Government acquires land with the ultimate purpose to transfer it for the use of private companies for stated public purpose. The purpose of LARR 2011 includes public-private-partnership projects, but excludes land acquired for state or national highway projects.
- Government acquires land for immediate and declared use by private companies for public purpose.

Here are Some Highlights of the Land Acquisition Bill, 2011

- The Bill provides for land acquisition as well as rehabilitation and resettlement. It replaces the Land Acquisition Act, 1894.
- The process for land acquisition involves a Social Impact Assessment survey, preliminary notification stating the intent for acquisition, a declaration of acquisition, and compensation to be given by a certain time. All acquisitions require rehabilitation and resettlement to be provided to the people affected by the acquisition.
- Without consent of Gram Sabhas no land can be acquired in Scheduled Areas.
- One should not be dispossess of the land till all the payments are made and alternative sites have been available.
- Compensation will be provided to those who are dependent on the land for their livelihood.
- In some cases where PPP projects are involved or private companies are taking acquisition, the Bill requires the consent of not less than 70 per cent and 80 per cent respectively (in both cases) of those whose land is sought to be acquired.

- To safeguard food security and to prevent arbitrary acquisition, the Bill directs States to impose limits on the area under agricultural cultivation that can be acquired.
- If land remains unutilised after acquisition, the new Bill empowers states to return the land either to the owner or to the State Land Bank.
- Where acquired land is sold to a third party for a higher price within three years of acquisition, then 40 per cent of the appreciated land value (or profit) will be shared with the original owners.
- The provisions of this Bill shall not apply to acquisitions under 16 existing legislations including the Special Economic Zones Act, 2005, the Atomic Energy Act, 1962, the Railways Act, 1989, etc.

Key Features

The Bill specifies provisions for land acquisition as well as R&R. Some of the major changes from the current provisions are related to–

(a) The process of land acquisition;
(b) Rights of the people displaced by the acquisition;
(c) Method of calculating compensation; and
(d) Requirement of R&R for all acquisitions.

Public Purpose

- Land may be acquired only for public purpose. The Bill defines public purpose to include: defence and national security; roads, railways, highways, and ports built by government and public sector enterprises The Bill defines "affected family" to include: (i) landowners; (ii) agricultural labourers, tenants who have been working in the affected area for three years prior to the acquisition; (iii) tribals and forest dwellers; (iv) families whose livelihood for the previous three years is dependent on the forests or water bodies; and (v) families who have been given land by the state or central government planned development and improvement of village or urban sites and residential purposes for the poor and landless, government administered schemes or institutions, etc. This is broadly similar to the provisions of the 1894 Act.

- In certain cases consent of 80 per cent of the project affected people is required to be obtained. These include acquisition of land for: (i) use by the government for purposes other than those mentioned above, and (ii) use by public-private partnerships, and (iii) use by private companies.

Process of Land Acquisition

- The government shall conduct a Social Impact Assessment (SIA) study, in consultation with the Gram Sabha in rural areas (and with equivalent bodies in case of urban areas). After this, the SIA report shall be evaluated by an expert group. The expert group shall comprise two non-official social scientists, two experts on rehabilitation, and a technical expert on the subject relating to the project. The SIA report will be examined further by a committee to ensure that the proposal for land acquisition meets certain specified conditions.
- A preliminary notification indicating the intent to acquire land must be issued within 12 months from the date of evaluation of the SIA Report. Subsequently, the government shall conduct a survey to determine the extent of land to be acquired. Any objections to this process shall be heard by the Collector. Following this, if the government is satisfied that a particular piece of land must be acquired for public purpose, a declaration to acquire the land is made. Once this declaration is published, the government shall acquire the land. No transactions shall be permitted for the specified land from the date of the preliminary notification until the process of acquisition is completed.
- In case of urgency, the above provisions are not mandatory. The urgency clause may be used only for defence, national security, and in the event of a natural calamity. Before taking possession of land in such cases, 80 per cent of the compensation must be paid.

Compensation to the Land Owners

The compensation for land acquisition is determined by the Collector and awarded by him to the land owner within two years from the date of publication of the declaration of acquisition. The process of determination of compensation is given below:

- First, the market value of the acquired land is computed as the higher of: (i) the land value specified in the Indian Stamp Act, 1899 for the registration of sale deeds; or (ii) the average of the top 50 per cent of all sale deeds in the previous three years for similar type of land situated in the vicinity.
- Once the market value is calculated, it is doubled for land in rural areas. There is no doubling of value in urban areas. Then, the value of all assets attached to the land (trees, buildings, etc.) is added to this amount. On this amount, a 100 per cent solatium, (i.e., extra compensation for the forcible nature of acquisition), shall be given to arrive at the final compensation figure.
- Land owners whose property is acquired using the urgency provisions shall be given an additional 75 per cent of the market value of the land.

Process of Rehabilitation and Resettlement

- The Bill requires R&R to be undertaken in case of every acquisition. Once the preliminary notification for acquisition is published, an Administrator shall be appointed. The Administrator shall conduct a survey and prepare the R&R scheme. This scheme shall then be discussed in the Gram Sabha in rural areas (equivalent bodies in case of urban areas). Any objections to the R&R scheme shall be heard by the Administrator. Subsequently, the Administrator shall prepare a report and submit it to the Collector. The Collector shall review the scheme and submit it to the Commissioner appointed for R&R. Once the Commissioner approves the R&R scheme, the government shall issue a declaration identifying the areas required for the purpose of R&R. The

Administrator shall then be responsible for the execution of the scheme. The Commissioner shall supervise the implementation of the scheme.

- In case of acquisition of more than 100 acres, an R&R Committee shall be established to monitor the implementation of the scheme at the project level. In addition, a National Monitoring Committee is appointed at the central level to oversee the implementation of the R&R scheme for all projects.
- In case the land is being privately purchased (100 acres in rural areas and 50 acres in urban areas), an application must be filed with the Collector who shall forward this to the Commissioner for approval. After the application has been approved, the Collector shall issue awards as per the R&R scheme.

Rehabilitation and Resettlement entitlements

- Every resettled area is to be provided with certain infrastructural facilities. These facilities include roads, drainage, provision for drinking water, grasing land, banks, post offices, public distribution outlets, etc.
- The Bill also provides the displaced families with certain R&R entitlements. These include, among other things: (i) land for a house as per the Indira Awas Yojana in rural areas or a constructed house of at least 50 square metres plinth area in urban areas; (ii) a one-time allowance of Rs 50,000 for affected families; and (iii) the option of choosing either mandatory employment in projects where jobs are being created or a one-time payment of Rs 5 lakh or an inflation adjusted annuity of Rs 2,000 per month per family for 20 years.

Other provisions

- A Land Acquisition and Rehabilitation and Resettlement Authority shall be established for settling any disputes relating to the process of acquisition, compensation, and R&R.

- There shall be no change of ownership of acquired land without prior permission from the government. Land may not be used for any purpose other than for which it is acquired.
- Acquired land which has been unused for 10 years from the date of possession shall be returned to the Land Bank of the government. If any unused acquired land is transferred to another individual, 20 per cent of the appreciated land value shall have to be shared amongst the original land owners.
- The government may temporarily occupy and use any piece of waste or arable land for a public purpose. This occupation may be for a period of not more than three years. The compensation of such land may be decided mutually by the owner of the land and the Collector. Any disagreement on matters relating to compensation or the condition of the land on being returned shall be referred to the Land Acquisition and R&R Authority.
- In any district, land acquisition will be restricted to a maximum of five per cent of irrigated multi-crop land.
- The provisions of this Bill shall not apply to land acquisition under 16 existing laws. These include: the SEZ Act, 2005, Atomic Energy Act, 1962 and the National Highways Act, 1956.

Comparison Between the 1894 Act and the 2011 Bill/LARR-2013

Issue	*1894 Act*	*2011 Bill/LARR-2013*
Public Purpose	Includes several uses such as infrastructure, development and housing projects. Also includes use by companies under certain conditions.	No significant change.
Consent from affected people	No requirement.	Consent of 80 per cent of displaced people required in case of acquisition for private companies and public-private partnerships.
SIA	No provision.	SIA has to be undertaken in case of every acquisition.

(*Contd...*)

Compensation	Based on the market value.	Market value doubled in rural areas and not in urban area.
Market Value	Based on the current use of land. Explicitly prohibits using the intended use of land while computing market value.	Higher of: (a) value specified for stamp duty, and (b) average of the top 50 per cent by recorded price of sale of land in the vicinity.
Solatium	30 per cent	100 per cent
Resale of land	No provision.	Prior permission of the government required.
Sharing of profit	No provision.	If the acquired land is unused and is transferred, 20 per cent of the profits shall be shared with the original land owners.
R&R	No provision for R&R.	R&R necessary for all affected families. Minimum R&R entitlements to be provided to each affected family specified.

Source- http://www.prsindia.org/uploads/media/Land%20and%20R%20and%20R/LARR%20-%20Final%20Brief.pdf

LARR (Amendment) Bill, 2015

The Right to Fair Compensation and Transparency in Land Acquisition, Rehabilitation and Resettlement (Amendment) Bill, 2015 was introduced in Lok Sabha on February 24, 2015. The following amendments were circulated by the government on March 9, 2015.

Change to public purpose

- The Bill amends the Act to include acquisition of land for private hospitals and private educational institutions within the definition of public purpose.
- The amendments remove this provision of the Bill. This implies that acquisition of land for private hospitals and private educational institutions is no longer included within the definition public purpose.

Changes to five categories of exempted projects

- The Bill allows the government to exempt five categories of projects from: (i) Social Impact Assessment, (ii) limits on acquisition of irrigated multi-cropped land, through a notification, and (iii) consent provisions. These five categories are: (i) defence, (ii) rural infrastructure,

(iii) affordable housing, (iv) industrial corridors, and (v) infrastructure and social infrastructure. The amendments make the following changes to this provision:

- Industrial corridors: The amendments clarify that land acquired for industrial corridors will be for industrial corridors set up by the government and government undertakings. Further, land can be acquired up to 1 km on both sides of the designated railway line or road of the industrial corridor.
- Social infrastructure: The amendments remove social infrastructure as an exempted category.

Changes to SIA and limits on irrigated multi-cropped land

The Bill allows the government to exempt the above five categories of projects from SIA and limits on irrigated land, through a notification. The amendments add that before issuing this notification, the government must ensure that the extent of land being acquired is in keeping with the minimum land required for such a project.

Survey of wasteland

The amendments add that the government must conduct a survey of its wasteland including arid land, and maintain a record containing details of such land, as may be prescribed by the government.

Changes to rehabilitation and resettlement:

- Under the Act, the rehabilitation and resettlement award for each affected family includes employment for at least one member of the family.
- The amendments change this provision to ensure compulsory employment to at least one member of such an 'affected family of a farm labourer'.

Changes to Land Acquisition, Rehabilitation and Resettlement Authority

- The Act provides for the establishment of a Land Acquisition, Rehabilitation and Resettlement (LARR) Authority which may be approached in case a person is not satisfied with an award under the Act.

- The amendments state that the LARR Authority must hold its hearing in the district where the land acquisition is taking place, after receiving a reference from the Collector and giving notice of this reference to all concerned parties.

Changes to application of 2013 Act

- The Land Acquisition Act, 1894 will continue to apply in certain cases, when an award has been made under it. The 2013 Act will apply in case an award has been made five years prior to the commencement of the 2013 Act but the physical possession of the land has not been taken or compensation has not been paid.
- The Bill states that in calculating the five year time period, any period where possession of land was taken but the compensation is lying deposited in a court or any account, will not be counted. The amendments change 'account' to 'designated account'.

Offences by government employees

- The Bill states that if an offence is committed by a government employee he cannot be prosecuted without the prior sanction of the government, as provided in Section 197 of the Code of Criminal Procedure, 1973.
- The amendments state that the government employee can be prosecuted if procedure laid down in Section 197 of the Code of Criminal Procedure, 1973 is followed. Section 197 requires the prior sanction of the government prior to prosecuting a public servant.

Comparison Between the LARR Act -2013 and LARR - (Amendment) Bill, 2015

LARR-ACT- 2013	*LARR - (AMENDMENT) BILL, 2015*
• Mandatory 70 per cent consent • Mandatory 80 per cent consent for private projects. • Mandatory Social impact assessment (SIA) for every projects.	Those "mandatory" things are no longer required for 5 types of projects: 1. National security and Defense Production 2. Rural infrastructure, Rural electrification 3. Infrastructure and Social infrastructure 4. Industrial corridors 5. Housing for Poors.
SIA mandatory for every type of project.	SIA not needed for 1. Those five categories listed above 2. PPP projects, IF Government owns the land. Building private hospitals and private educational institutes will also count as "public purpose". Means, they too can acquire land if 80 per cent affected families agreed.
Compensation: 1. 4 times the market rate in rural area. 2. 2 times in urban area.	Remains the same.
Stringent provisions for relief and rehabilitation (R&R).	Remains the same.
Private "**companies**" can acquire land for public purpose.	Private "**entities**" can acquire. Meaning private companies, NGOs, trusts, foundations, charity bodies, proprietors etc. too can acquire land for "public purpose".
If any mischief played on Government's part then head of the department will be responsible.	• Head of the department can't be prosecuted without prior sanction of government (under CrPC Section 197). • This "immunity" is given to ensure bureaucrats don't sit on the files, fearing media-trials and judicial activism.

Source:- http://mrunal.org/2015/01/polity-land-ordinance-features-criticism-land-acquisition.html

Notes

1. Indian Institute of Technology Roorkee, *Development Projects vs. Internally Displaced Populations in India: A Literature Based Appraisal,* February 2011, p. 6.
2. Cernea, M.M. (ed.) 1999. The Economics of Involuntary Resettlement: Questions and Challenges, World Bank, Washington, D.C.
3. Cernea. Michael M. 2006. Foreword: Ethics and Economics in Resettlement Policy and Practice. In Shobita Jain and Madhubala (eds), *The Economics and Politics of Resettlement in India.* New Delhi: Longman, pp.xii-xxi.
4. Fernades, Walter and A.Raj. 1992. *Development, Displacement and Rehabilitation in the Tribal Areas of Orissa.* Report, Indian Social Institute, New Delhi.
5. Ganguly Thukral, Enakshi and Mridula Singh. 1995. ' Dams and the Displaced in India', in Harimohan Mathur (ed.), *Development, Displacement and Resettlement: Focus on Asia.* New Delhi: Vikash Publishing Company, pp. 93-121.
6. Fernandes, Walter 1998b. The Land Acquisition (Amendment) Bill 1998: Rights of the Project Affected Persons Ignored. *Economic and Political Weekly* 33 (42-43), pp. 2703-2706.
7. Fernandes, Walter and S. Anthony Raj 1992. *Development, Displacement and Rehabilitation in the Tribal Areas of Orissa.* Indian Social Institute: New Delhi.
8. Pattanaik, Gopabandhu and Damodar Panda 1992. *The New Economic Policy and the Poor. Social Action,* 42(2), pp.201-212.
9. Pandey, Balaji 1998. *Displacement Development, Impact of Open Cast Mining on Women.* Friedrich Ebert Stiftung: New Delhi.
10. Fernandes, Walter (et al) 2001: *Development Induced Displacement in Andhra Pradesh,* 1951-1995. A Quantitative and Qualitative Study of its Extent and Nature. Indian Social Institute: New Delhi (mimeographed).
11. Yugandhar, B.N. 1998. Land Acquisition for Non-existent Aliminium Projects: Experiences of Displacement of Tribals in the Scheduled Area of Orissa. *Journal of Management* 28(1).
12. Singh, Mridula 1992. *Displacement by Sardar Sarovar and Tehri, A Comparative Study of Two Dams.*

13. Gajrajan, C.S. 1970. *Planned Rehabilitation and Economic Change: A Case Study of Tungabhadra River Project Rehabilitation Colonised at H.B. Halli.* Gokhale Institute of Economics and Politics: Poona.
14. Mathur, Hari Mohan and Marsden 1998. *Development Projects and Impoverishment Risks, resettling project-affected people in India.* Oxford University Press: New Delhi.
15. Jain, Shobhita 1995. Habitat, Human Displacement and Development Cost: A Case Study. *Social Action* 45, pp. 299-317.
16. Mathur, Hari Mohan and Marsden 1998. *Development Projects and Impoverishment Risks, resettling project-affected people in India.* Oxford University Press: New Delhi.
17. Pandey, Balaji 1998. *Displacement Development, Impact of Open Cast Mining on Women.* Friedrich Ebert Stiftung: New Delhi.
18. Mathur, Hari Mohan and Marsden 1998. *Development Projects and Impoverishment Risks, resettling project-affected people in India.* Oxford University Press: New Delhi.
19. Areeparampil, Mathew 1989. Industries, Mines. and Dispossession of Indigenous Peoples: The Case of Chhottanagpur in Walter Fernandes and E.G. Thukral (ed s.) *Development, Displacement and Rehabilitation.* Indian Social Institute: New Delhi.
20. Vidyarthi, L.P. 1970. *Socio-Cultural Implications of Industrialisation in India - A Case Study of Tribal Bihar Research Programme Committee.* Planning Commission: New Delhi.
21. Saxena, N.C. 2006. *The Resettlement and Rehabilitation Policy of India'* In Hari Mohan Mathur (eds), *Managing Resettlement in India - Approaches, Issues, Experiences.* Oxford University Press: New Delhi.

Websites

http://www.prsindia.org/uploads/media/Land%20and%20R%20and%20R/LARR%20 %20Final%20Brief.pdf

http://mrunal.org/2015/01/polity-land-ordinance-features-criticism-land-acquisition.html

Chapter 3

An Indian State Scenario

An Indian State, Odisha, occupies a unique place among the underdeveloped states of India because of its large concentration of Tribal population. The most striking fact about Odisha is that while it is rich in resource, its people are extremely poor. Odisha, though a relatively backward state in term of standard of living indicators, possesses a vast amount of mineral, water and forest resources. The state is richly endowed with minerals like coal, iron ore, bauxites, chromites, manganese ore, graphite and rare earth, etc. Being a land of rivers, Odisha has a vast potential of water resource, which can be harnessed for irrigation, power generation, and provision of drinking water in rural areas. Yet, it remains one of the most drought prone state in the country. The bulk of this potential of water resource is utilised by multi purpose or major and medium dam projects. At the same time, the availability of rich minerals of different varieties in the region has also encouraged the growth of large-scale industrial and mining projects in the state.

Although development activities in Odisha began in the late forties, it gained real momentum in the early fifties after independence with the introduction planned development. The notable projects in the fifties were the Rourkela Steel Plant and Hirakud Multi purpose Dam. The Hindustan Aeronautics Limited (HAL), Talcher Thermal Power Station (TTPS) and the Balimela Dam came in the Sixties. The Seventies saw the establishment of the Rengali, Upper Kolab, Upper Indravati and Subernarekha Multi Purpose Dams. The Ib Thermal Power Station (ITPS), Talcher Super Thermal Power Projects and the National Aluminium Company (NALCO) were set up in the eighties. Along with these mega projects, open cast mining operations also begun in the state from the Sixties. All these resulted in large-scale appropriation of land- mainly agriculture land. These projects were executed in resource- rich regions, which had been inhabited for generation by the tribal and the rural poor. Though these development projects indeed brought manifold benefits to the state, there is a flip side to it. None can deny that they have also lead to large-scale displacement of people in the resource- rich interior areas. This was due to encroachment on land not only for extraction of raw materials, but also for the establishment of factories, reservoirs and residential complex. The indirect consequence of these activities had been the destruction of the habitat of the rural poor and the loss of their means of livelihood, which was mainly agriculture and utilisation and sale of forest produce. The groups displaced were mostly the weaker sections of society belonging to the Scheduled Caste, Scheduled Tribes and Other Backward Classes.

Development Scenario

The state of Odisha in the east coast of Indian sub-continent, comprises of 4.74 per cent of the total land mass, and has an area about 155, 707 Sq Km². Odisha extends from 17° 49 N to 22° 34 N latitude and from 81° 29E to 87° 29E longitude on the eastern coast of India. It is bounded by West Bengal in the north-east, Chhattisgarh in the west, Jharkhand in the north, Andhra Pradesh in the south and the Bay of Bengal in the east. While more than two-thirds of the area is comprised of hilly forest, it has a coastline of 480 Kms. The state was formed in 1936 as a single linguistic entity with 13 districts, presently there are 30 districts in the state with the city of Bhubaneswar as its capital. Odisha is divided into three revenue divisions: Central, Southern and Northern. According to the 2001 Census records the total population of Odisha was 368, 05 lakh which constitute 3.58 per cent of the total population of the country. Odisha is one of the most backward states in India with a diverse composition. Odisha has been suffering from regional disparities and inequality despite many development projects and programmes. Even more than six decades after independence, some of the regions of this state are very backward and constitutes the largest proportion of poor in the country. The challenges rose by intra-regional disparities and their compounding implications on living conditions and governance are enormous. Odisha is marked as much by disparities within the state, as by absolute deprivation. The regional disparities are substantial, appear mostly multi-dimensional, and have shown little signs of being reduced. The overall economy in Odisha remains backward through it is rich in natural resource potential. The apparent reasons of underdevelopment in Odisha are conditioned historically. Prior to 1930s the Odisha speaking population was scattered under different presidencies, and it was only in 1936 a separate Odisha province came into being.

Nearly 85 per cent of population of Odisha lives in rural areas and depends mostly on agriculture for their livelihood, whereas, urban population constitutes 15 per cent. Agriculture being the source of income and employment for 85 per cent of its people has never got priority. Officially, only about 34 per cent of the irrigable land benefits from irrigation facilities'. Hence, in hill forested tracts, rain fed agriculture and forest collection are the primary source of livelihood. About 45 per cent of the total area in the state is declared as Scheduled Area under the Fifth Schedule of the Constitution. The forest area in the state is 9963, 30 sq. km constituting 38 per cent of the total area. The cultivable land in Odisha has declined. In between 1980-2000, 26,500 hectares of forest land were destroyed for mines and industries. In 1980s, 63 lakh hectares of land used for cultivation declined to 57 lakh hectares in 2005.

As in any developing economy, the economy of Odisha has been going through structural changes away from agriculture in favour of industry and services. In the pursuit of growth based on a neo-liberal development paradigm in an era of heightened economic globalisation, the Odisha state government has favoured increased foreign direct investment in the development project and has relied significantly on the exploitation of natural resources for export at the expense of environmental and local communities. The state is endowed with huge water and mineral resources having about a third of the country's iron ore reserves, large bauxite, chromate, coal and dolomite. Thus, the state government has emphasised strongly on industrialisation of the state to eradicate poverty, to open up employment opportunities to be educated and un-skilled labour, besides enhancing the state's revenue. The elites of Odisha, mainly politicians, higher caste land owners, traders and the urban middle class have always taken a pro-industry stand for rapid industrialisation. In the general elections, both national and regional, political parties of the state have been giving false promises to provide jobs to growing number of unemployed educated youths. It may be recalled in early 1980s when the first case of child sale due to hunger and starvation was reported from Kalahandi, the then Chief Minister of Odisha announced 1000 industries in 1000 days to be set up. The public sector mega Aluminum plants were set up in Anugul and Koraput districts in the early 1980s. These two industries displaced more people than jobs provided. The displaced families got promises of employment but only of a few got lower grade jobs. The local political lobby recruits people of their choice, not the local displaced people. The state's new industrial policy is committed to radical reforms in the laws and rules guiding labour and employment, creation of employment opportunities, establishment of globally-competitive industry, restructuring of industry in line with changing market conditions and deter investment. The state's endeavours aimed at encouraging private investment at any cost have been vigorous. During the last Ten years, the state government has signed 43 memorandums of understanding (MoUs). Notable among them are international and Indian corporate giants, namely POSCO (Korea), Vedanta Aluminum (UK), Rio Tinto (UK), BHP Billition (UK-Australia), Alcan (Canada), Hindalco, Jindal, Tata and Sterlite. Mining projects worth 3,000 billion rupees have already been launched and projects worth a further. 11, 000 billion rupees are in the pipeline. The state also proposes to build two more ports in Dhamara and Gopalpur to provide investors with a gateway to international trade. The state has given lease to 18 rivers and reservoirs for exclusive use by industry for its water intensive activities. Thus, Odisha is fast emerging as a major site of foreign direct investment and multinational development projects, which violates the rights of the indigenous population in the hill districts and mineral reserves areas of Odisha.

The corporate houses claim that they will share the responsibility of livelihood and social security of the displaced people but this has not happened. It is estimated that some 3 to 5 million people have been displaced since 1950 in Odisha on account of various development projects, of which more than 50 per cent are tribal's, and the expected displacement in the coming decades also is expected to affect tribal's disproportionally. The process of development has reduced them to ecological refugees, victims of strategy growth and the promise of employment and prosperity has remained elusive. The continuing disparities between social groups also appear the result of social practices of discrimination, and that development has not reached remote areas and tribal groups. The history of displacement and lack of adequate resettlement and rehabilitation similarly illustrates that deprivation has been the result of exploitative social and economic processes.

Irrigation and Hydro Power (Dam) Projects

The interstate Machhkund Hydel Project on river Duduma in Koraput District was the first major reservoir in Odisha. Conceived by the Maharaja of Jeypore, and followed by a two decade long planning, it was finally launched in 1948. The initial phase of the construction of the dam was marked by the displacement of 2,938 families from the area by 1960. Of these families 1500 (51 per cent) were Tribals and 300 (10.21 per cent) belonged to the Scheduled Caste (Mahapatra 1990). The projects also caused submergence of 14000 acres of private land 6100 acre (2469.62 ha) belonged to tribals, 1700 acres (688.26ha) to Scheduled Caste and the remaining 6100 acre (2469.63 ha) to other communities[1].

The Hirakud Multipurpose river valley project on the river Mahanadi in Sambalpur district was the first major project to be conceived after independence. Construction work on this Rs 478 million project started in 1948. By the time it was completed in 1957 almost Rs 851 Million had been spent on it.[2] The project was set up with the aim of solving some of Odisha's major problems namely floods, droughts, poverties and diseases. Flood control, irrigation, hydel power generation, navigation and fishing activity were the thrust areas in the planning and designing of the project reports. The main purpose for the construction of the dam was to facilitate intensive cultivation, extension cultivable land, increased productivity, security against uncertainty and loss in agriculture, new efficient agriculture parties and optimum utilisation of various types of land, crop diversification, employment generation, large scale industrialisation etc. The construction of the Dam affected 285 villages of which

249 villages (108 fully and 141 partly affected) in Odisha, and 36 villages (3 fully and 33 partly affected) in Madhya Pradesh[3]. It displaced or disrupted the livelihood of 22,144 families consists of about 110,000 people (Government of Odisha 1968).

The Balimela Multipurpose Dam project on Seleru river at Chitrakonda in the then undivided Koraput district is another inter-state project which was undertaken as a joint venture by Odisha and Andhra Pradesh on a 50:50 share basis. Work started on the project in 1960-63 and it was completed in 1977 incurring an expenditure of 563 million. The project resulted in the submergence of 17496 ha of land in Odisha and 648 ha in Andhra Pradesh and nearly 2000 families were displaced[4].

The Rengali Multipurpose river valley project on the Brahmani in the Angul district on which work begun in 1973 and which was completed in 1992-93 incurred an expenditure of little over Rs 2900 million. The project was designed to control flood, generate power as per installed capacity of 250 MW and firm capacity of 151MW and provide irrigation to 4,23,000 ha of land in the then undivided Dhenkanal, Keonjhar and Cuttack District. The reservoir created under the project submerged 4,14,500 ha of land and 249 village were displaced (Dalua 1991). Out of the 10897 families displaced 1710 (15.69 per cent) belonged to SCs, 1172 (10.75 per cent) were Tribals and the rest came from other communities[5].

Industrial Projects

Odisha is rich in mineral resources; it attracted a large number of industries to the state. There are major industrial projects- the Rourkela Steel Plant and the National Aluminium Company, the fertiliser Corporation of India (FCI) at Talcher, Hindustan Aeronautics Ltd. (HAL) etc. Due to liberalisation of economy in 1991, many industries came to the State. The Land Acquisition work for most of the projects is in progress. Due to the concentration of mineral deposits in tribal belt, most of the industries have come up in this area. As a result of these industrial activities, the tribals are not only facing thousands of outsiders who have intruded into their socio-economic environment and they have also displaced from their home and become landless and unemployed. The Rourkela Steel Plant, the NALCO, the HAL and the Saintala Ordnance Factory, which have been led to large-scale displacement.

In the aegis of neoliberal development strategies, one primary factor of production i.e. land has become the centre of discussion among policy makers, bureaucrats, academic and researchers more than any other factor. Above all the common people have come to focus their attention to it than ever before. The unlimited desire of the capitalist to acquire land by any means has become the centre of controversy at different parts of the country at different time period. The development paradigm considers mega projects and large dams as the inevitable way for the development and the synonymous of development. The coalition between capitalist, politicians, bureaucrats, contractors and pressure from urban consumers used to push for the adoption of these mega projects which require large land area and causes large scale population displacement. The snatching away of land and common property resources (CPR) from the people living in the interior parts of the State severely affects and dismantles the life and livelihood of the people who are adversely affected by these projects. These big projects are embedded with huge social cost which in very often get neglected in the face of present state of development paradigm. When the life and livelihood of affected population are at stake it is obvious that projects are bound to be protested by the people and even be stalled.

Instruments of Land Acquisition

Development projects demand for acquisition of land. Land is acquired by the government under the colonial Land Acquisition Act, (LAA) 1894 on eminent domain and public purpose. The British were all set to modernise the then capital city, Calcutta but they were ill equipped, without acquiring the state rights over individual land. The first All India Act VI of 1857 was passed where land owners may be required by the legislature to surrender some of their rights they possess over their land for a purpose of public utility. Subsequently, a well defined, all Comprehensive Land Acquisition Act (LAA) covering the whole of British India came into force on the first day of March, 1894 as the Act 1 of 1894. Under the clause of 'Eminent Domain' and 'Public Purpose' the state is empowered to acquire privately owned land. Till now with minor amendments in 1984 this

Act is being followed by the State as well as Government of India in the matter of land acquisition and distribution of compensation to the land owner. The mode of compensation is based on the market value of land only. The legal holders are only entitled to get the compensation on the basis of a land valuation fixed by the government taking note in to the sale deeds of that area. The valuation as fixed by the LAA fails to take in to consideration the future returns of land and which is usually less than the replacement cost of land. Another important dimension of land acquisition is that those people having land record of rights are accounted and people having no title to land rights and dependants on Common Property Resources (CPRs) are discounted from the purview of the act.

In addition to the LAA1894 there are 16 more Central Acts which causes land acquisition and displacement. These are namely; The Land Acquisition (Mines) Act, 1885, The Indian Tramways Act, 1886, The Works of Defence Act, 1903, The Forest Act, 1927, The Manoeuvre, Field Firing and Artillery Practice Act, 1938, The Resettlement of Displaced Persons (Land Acquisition) Act, 1948, The Damodar Valley Corporation Act, 1948, The Requisitioning and Acquisition of Immovable Property Act, 1952, The National Highway Act, 1956. The Coal Bearing Areas Acquisition and Development Act, 1957, The Ancient Monuments and Archaeological Sites and Remains Act, 1958, The Atomic Energy Act, 1962, The Petroleum and Minerals Pipelines (Acquisition of Right of User in Land) Act, 1962, The Metro Railways (Construction of Works) Act, 1978, The Railway Act, 1989, The Electricity Act, 2003, The Special Economic Zones Act, 2005, the Cantonments Act, 2006, and the Special Economic Zones Act, 2005. It is generally regarded land as state subject, the state face the wrath of people in the form of protest movement. But land can be acquired by the Union as well as State government for different purposes.

After industrialisation gathered momentum, particularly with the on set New Economic Policy 1991, private companies both domestic and foreign entered the race for getting hold of land in various parts of the country. They themselves entered the land market and started acquiring land at the prevailing market price. But what became more treacherous, the State became an agent for the private sector in the name of industrialisation and higher Gross Domestic Product (GDP).

Liberal Economic Policy has led much more land acquisition and displacement than was practiced in the past, especially in states that already have a high number of previous displaced people/project affected people but promised large tracts of land for Special Economic Zones (SEZ). For example, Odisha used 98,000 acres for industries in 1951-95 and plan to acquire 98,000 acres more in the succeeding decade[6]. The intense controversies over land acquisition and displacement for the last several decades have compelled the Government of India to go for a new law. The new Land Acquisition and Resettlement & Rehabilitation (R&R) Bill 2011, is going to take the issue of R&R along with land acquisition. The new law is likely to address the problem of land acquisition and displacement in a progressive manner then earlier.

Odisha is a state of two in one. Geographically the state has been divided into hill districts of Western Odisha and coastal districts of plain. The coastal districts of Odisha compared to the hill or Western districts are in a much more advantageous and privileged state both in political and economic aspects. In view of large mineral deposits, a number of large scale industries have developed in this area – such as the aluminium industries at Angul, Damanjodi; the Hindustan Aeronautic Ltd. at Sunabeda; the Steel Plant at Rourkela; Cement plants at Bargarh, Jharsuguda and Rajgangpur; ordnance factory at Saintala; Refractory at Belpahar and Rajgangpur; Thermal power stations at Banharpali. In the 1950s, one of the world's largest artificial lakes i.e. Hirakud Dam near Sambalpur has been built across the river Mahanadi. All these projects have acquired large scale cultivable land and forest land and caused large scale population displacement.

Extent of Displacement

Land acquisition coexists with the evils of population displacement. Researchers like Professor. M. Cernea, Walter Fernandes and others have tried to evolve a data base for the displaced people of different projects in India. In India, of the 20 million people displaced since 1947, it is estimated that 75 per cent of them have been impoverished due to development projects.[7] During the last two decades of the previous century, the magnitude of force population displacement caused by development programme was of the order of 10 million people each year or some 200 million people globally during that period.[8]

Table 3.1: A Conservative Estimate of Displaced Persons by various categories of Projects India (1951-1990)

Sl. No.	*Type of Project*	*Number of Displaced*	*Number of Rehabilitated*	*Back log*
1.	Dams	1,64,00,000	41,00,000	1,23,00,000
2.	Mines	25,50,000	6,30,000	19,20,000
3.	Industries	12,50,000	3,75,000	8,75,000
4.	Sanctuaries	6,00,000	1,25,500	4,75,000
5.	Others	5,00,000	1,50,000	3,50,000
	Total	**2,13,00,000**	**53,80,000**	**1,59,20,000**

Source: Fernandez and *et. al.,* 1998, p. 251.

The above table 3.1 shows the number of displaced people in the country during 1951-90 in India. Among all the displacing projects, dams top the list. and Table 2 shows a few cases of displacement situation of West Odisha.

Table 3.2

Name of Project	*Total land Acquired in Acre*	*No. of villages Affected*	*No. of families Affected*	*No. of People Displaced*
Hirakud Dam	167,377	249	22,144	160,000
Upper Indravati Dam	32477	105	5301	18,500
Rengali Dam	102,672	263	11,289	46,570
Rourkela Steel Plant	19,277	30	4251	23,400
Bhusan Steel	1315	13	164	854
IB Thermal Power Station	487	03	147	748
Ib Valley Open Coal mine	4500	18	110	495
OCL India, Rajgangpur	1133	—	13	105
VAL, Lanjigarh	1516	—	1248	600
Upper Kolab Dam	28375	49	3179	15,890

Sources: Reddy, 1992, p. 176, B. Pandey, 1998, Sabar, 2010 and Other Official Records, 2007.

The above table shows cases of displacement & amount of land acquisition for a few selected public sector projects and private industries established during the pre and post reform periods. In this context it may be said that while acquiring land the quality and the need aspect of land is not taken into consideration. For Hirakud reservoir project there was acquisition of 1,67,377 acre but it lost good quality land amounting to 1,15,128 acre in the reservoir forever.

There is an excess acquisition of land by number of projects only in the name of development. This is going to threaten the food security in future. With the adoption of New Economic Policy 1991, the domestic private sector and multinationals have assume the role of industrialising the state mainly through the mineral based industries rather than through any value additive industries. Other groups such as Bhusan, Vedanta, Aditya Birla are going to add more to land acquisition and displacement through their mining and industrial operation in Western Odisha. The controversy over Vedanta's mining in Niyamgiri has shown the aggressive capitalism for the use of natural resources in west Odisha. According to latest information 10,226.437 hectares of forest land have been diverted for mines, industries and infrastructure projects in the state. Out of which the share of forest land diverted for such purposes in west Odisha is 3718.281 hectares.[9]

The Kalinga Nagar Industrial Complex

The Government of Odisha mooted the idea of developing a major industrial complex in the early nineties of the twentieth century in the mineral-rich region of Dangadi, Duburi and Sukinda located in the district of Jajpur. The proposed complex has the capacity of producing 15 million tons of steel annually. The complex includes about 13 mineral-based industries such as iron and steel, stainless steel, sponge iron and ferrochrome etc. Iron ore and chromites are the raw materials for these industries, which are available in plenty in the region. The state government has already signed a Memorandum of Understanding with nearly ten units spread over an area of 13,000 hectares. The major corporate houses such as the Tatas, Visa, Jindal, Mesco and some others have already started their projects and a few of them are nearing completion. In pursuance of the MOU, the state government would grant mining lease to the concerned industrial units and provide them with land for setting up their industries.

Further, the state government has agreed to acquire land from the local residents as well as to look into all matters relating to displacement, rehabilitation, and resettlement. However, all the efforts for industrialisation are met with violent protest movements with increasing frequency. The tribal people inhabiting the region have repeatedly expressed their dissatisfaction over the payment of compensation, which ultimately resulted in loss of life of 13 persons who were from among the tribal community on January 2, 2006 .In the encounter that ensued between the police and the displaced people one Police Havildar was killed and four policemen were seriously injured while the compound wall of the 15,500 crore steel plant of the Tata was under construction.

The compensation package was announced in 1994, according to which a land oustee was to be paid at the rate of Rs 35000 per acre through the Industrial Development Corporation (IDCO), a corporation of the Government of Odisha. Mediating between the State Government and the displaced people, the IDCO sold the land to the industrial houses at a rate of Rs 1,00,000 per acre. The compensation package was revised later in order to enhance the rate of compensation to Rs 50,000 per acre. The people complained that they were paid less and being forced to lose their means of livelihood. The unfortunate incident of loss of lives of 13 persons not only united the tribal communities of the state but also attracted the sympathy and support of the tribal people from outside the state, giving rise to a complicated political situation and completely stalling the construction work of the industrial unit. The growth of pan-tribal unity is an emerging political phenomenon against the state political leadership.

Since January 2, 2006, the tribals of Kalinga Nagar started launched an indefinite economic blockade on the National Highway 200 at Madhuban Chhak. They are not prepared to work out any compromise with the State Government. So far all efforts of the government to appease the tribes have failed, and the present situation is characterised by a deep emotional overtone. The place where the 13 victims of police firing were cremated has been named as Bir Bhumi and on May 23, about 5000 women from Odisha, Chhattisgarh, Jharkhand and Andhra Pradesh took out a rally and resolved not to lift the road blockade. Among other things the 7-point charter of demands of the Bistapan Birodhi Janamanch includes a complete halt to displacement in the area. The economic blockade has drawn the attention of the judiciary which has issued direction to the state government to take suitable steps to lift it as early as possible. The road blockade continued for more than four years.

When the political climate is heavily charged with anti-government slogans and an unprecedented unity among the tribes of the state and of the neighbouring states has emerged as a strong political force, the Tata Steel Company has announced a package. The package, it seems, is an act of wisdom on the part of the concerned corporate house. According to the scheme, every displaced family would be considered as a family of the Tata Steel and the Company would look into their all-round development. The Company would take stock of the social and economic conditions of the displaced families every month and all the families numbering about 700 would be provided with identity cards and their progress in matters of rehabilitation and resettlement would be monitored regularly. Further, the Company would give employment benefit to all the displaced families and also revise the compensation package after proper negotiation with the people .The Company has formed a task force which includes 7 tribal members to look into all matters relating to displacement and resettlement. The package, it is claimed, is the best in the country.

Protest against the Vedanta Alumina Limited, Lanjigarh

The Niyamgiri Hill of Kalahandi district has a bauxite deposit of 1950 lakh tons. The district of Kalahandi is one of the least industrially developed parts of the country. In view of its special characteristics of backwardness, a special project of the central government called KBK (Kalahandi, Balangir, and Koraput) covering three former backward districts of Odisha is under implementation. In the recent past, the district attracted a lot of attention of the media due to outbreak of famine conditions, drought and incidence of extreme poverty of the masses leading to sale of babies. The district has a sizable population of the SCs, STs and OBCs.

Recently, the Vedanta Alumina Limited has started its work for setting up a plant at Lanjigarh and mining of bauxite from the Niyamgiri Hill complex. While efforts are being made to change a predominantly rural economy and hilly area into a major industrial complex, the people have been strongly resisting the work of setting up of the plant and mining of bauxite. A mass movement is going on since 2004. On April 7,2004 the Niyamgiri Suraksha Samiti, an organisation of one thousand tribal people of the area was formed to protect the forest, land and water of the area, giving the slogan, 'Vendat Hatao' (Remove Vendant).The people's cause has been taken up by another organisation known as the Green Kalahandi. The 'Niyamgiri Suraksha Samity' has been formed by the people to resist leasing out of the hills to the company on the ground of protecting the environment. The Niyamgiri has a number of perennial hill streams, which are useful for agriculture and for the purpose of drinking water of the tribal people living in the foothills. It is also the source of the river Bansadhara that flows through Andhra Pradesh. The hill is a place of worship of the people belonging to the Khond tribe.

The people of two villages namely, Kinari and Bolbhatta displaced and resettled in the foothill of Niyamgiri are not at all pleased in their new environment .The people protest against the use of ground water by the Company in a drought-prone area. For their cause, they have also sought the participation of political leaders of the neighbouring Andhra Pradesh. The local Congress leaders and the CPM are active in the movement. The agitating masses point out that the company has a plan of giving employment benefit to only 286 persons and the use of water from the river Tel by the company would spell disaster for the cultivating class of the district, besides causing environmental degradation.

The proposed Alumina project by the Vedanta group in Lanjigarh has provoked a political controversy between the ruling BJD and the opposition Congress. 'While the supporters of the BJD claim that the project will not only bring development in the area but will also generate employment', the opposition points out the possible adverse impact on Niyamgiri's bio-diversity. The reports by a Supreme Court committee and different scientific organisations have worked out the adverse implications of the project. A tribal leader and President of the Niyamgiri Suraksha Samiti Daisingh Majhi says: 'Niyamgiri hills, popularly called Niyam Penu (God) are considered as the mother of the tribals. Such emotional issues should be kept above petty politics'. Further he adds; the tribals are bothered about the area's forests, natural springs and wildlife resources. The parties should not indulge in politics over the nature's gift.

On April 18 2013, the Supreme Court put the fate of Vedanta's bauxite minining project in Odisha in the hands of people. It asked gram sabhas of the affected villages in Rayagada and Kalahandi districts to decide whether the tribals living in and around Niyamgiri hills have religious rights over it. Their "rights have to be preserved and protected", it said.

The Odisha Mining Corporation Limited (OMC) and Sterlite Industries, the Indian arm of Vedanta, propose to mine bauxite from 660 hectares (ha) of forestland on Niyamgiri for Vedanta's alumina refinery in nearby Lanjigarh. Though the Ministry of Environment and Forests (MoEF) gave preliminary clearance to the project, it quashed the approval in 2010, saying the project violated provisions of the Forest Conservation Act, Environment Protection Act and the Forest Rights Act (FRA). It also contended that the project violated religious rights of the Dongria Kondh and Kutia Kandha who worship the hill top of Niyamgiri as the abode of their deity Niyam Raja. In 2011, OMC challenged the decision in the apex court. The court observed while gram sabhas have settled most individual and community claims under FRA, the matter of religious rights was not properly placed before them. The gram sabhas will give their views on religious rights in three months, based on which MoEF will decide whether to grant stage-II clearance to the project. The gram sabhas can also consider fresh claims under FRA. To ensure that gram sabha proceedings are not influenced by project proponents, the state government or the Centre, the court directed that the proceedings be recorded in the presence of a judicial officer of the rank of district judge.

The court also directed Vedanta's alumina refinery project to correct the alleged violations in terms of environment clearance.

All the twelve affected gram sabhas in the region rejected the mining project one after the other in August 2013. Five months after the gram sabhas of tribal villages in Odisha's Niyamgiri hills rejected multinational company Vedanta's proposal to undertake bauxite mining in the area, the Union Ministry of Environment and Forests (MoEF) has said a final "no" to the project. The ministry has reiterated its stand that mining cannot be allowed on the Niyamgiri hills because it will affect the rights of the Dongria Kondhs, a particularly vulnerable tribal community that worships the Niyamgiri hills as its deity.

BALCO

The mining of bauxite in Odisha has given rise to virulent mass movements in the past. In the eighties of the past century, a strong movement of the local people completely stalled the mining activities of the Bharat Aluminium Company (BALCO), a Government of India undertaking with foreign technical collaboration. The BALCO initiated officially its mining work on May 2, 1983 that was scheduled to be completed by April, 1985. The project came to a grinding halt due to mass based agitations of the local people, mostly tribals despite the fact that the BALCO claimed to have invested 30 crores rupees on the project. The people have raised a number of significant questions relating to their development. Starting with purely religious demands, their movement came to embrace secular matters such as environmental protection, ecological balance and eradication of poverty in a perpetually drought-prone area. Incidentally, the BALCO has been sold to Sterlite/Vedant. The proposed steel project of the Tisco at Gopalpur, which involved acquisition of 3500 acres of land, and displacement of over 2000 people in the late Nineties, met the same fate. It appears history is being repeated.

Protest against POSCO Steel Plant at Jagatsinghpur

The people of Jagatsinghpur district in coastal Odisha have been actively engaged in a protest movement against Posco, a South Korean company planning to set up its 52000-crore steel plant since June' 2005. The company has also a plan to open a new private port of its own in order to avail the facilities of special economic zone. The Posco Pratirodh Sangram Samiti, an organisation of the local people, has been spearheading the movement.

The people living in 22 villages of three gram panchayats of Ersama block situated in the Ersamma Assembly constituency are likely to be displaced after the work starts. The memorandum of understanding with the South Korean major was signed on June 22, 2005 by the state government. It is proposed that the company would be given mining lease of 600 million tons of iron ore for which a separate MOU has to be signed, even to the extent of permitting the company to export iron ore. Further the state government would acquire 435 acres of private land for the plant which involves displacement of 20,000 to 25,000 of people. Since then the villagers of three gram panchayats such as Kujang, Dhinkia and Nuagaon have been restive over the issue. The Samiti has raised a brigade of 1200 people who are ready to keep the movement alive. At times there have been violent clashes between the supporters of the proposed plant and the people, calling for intervention of the police.

In one such incident which took place on 11 April, 2006, at Dhinkia village 11 persons were injured and nine activists were rounded off by the police. The people also complain against police excesses committed at the behest of the state government. More than 30,000 people have pledged not to obey any rule which the state government may enforce, pressing for their displacement. The Sangram Samiti has also involved the children and women of the locality. They have put up barricades at the entry points to these villages which are guarded by women and children to prevent entry of government and POSCO officials.

Political parties such as the Congress, the CPI, the CPM have been extending support to the people. On 22 June, 2006, as many as 20,000 people including 3,000 children decided to observe mass fasting to protest against their displacement. In view of the people's agitations the setting up of the plant is running behind the schedule. Despite the announcement made by the POSCO officials to the effect that the proposed plant would recruit 97 per cent Indians in its labour intensive project and would extend employment benefits to 48000 people directly, the people have turned a deaf ear to it. They strongly object to the setting up of the plant on several grounds.

Firstly, the phoenix method to be applied by the company for melting iron would adversely affect the environment for which no industrial house has obtained permission throughout the country.

Secondly, the huge quantity of water which would be utilised by the proposed plant from the river Mahanadi would not only affect the cultivators but also rob the fishing folk of their only means of livelihood. It is estimated that the number of project affected people is likely to cross one lakh.

Thirdly; the question of giving mining lease to a foreign company at a cheap rate has stirred up patriotic feelings among the people. It has been pointed out that the Government of Odisha would lose one lakh and thirty two thousand crores of rupees in the event of granting lease of the iron ore to the company. The Hind Majdoor Sabha has expressed its deep concern over the proposal to set up a new private port by the POSCO since it would affect the working of the existing Para dip port. The Sangram Samiti has raised a band of young men who are prepared even to sacrifice their lives in resisting the move for displacement.

The steel giant POSCO has waited for this 12 million tonne per annum (MTPA) port-based steel plant to take off for nearly a decade. But recently with the Centre ruling out any out of turn allocation of iron ore mines to the company and the Odisha government giving the impression of washing its hands of the project, the steel major's patience appears to be wearing thin in 2015. Nothing proves this exasperation better than the ugly war of words between POSCO and Industrial Infrastructure Development Corporation of Odisha (IDCO), the land acquisition arm of the state government. In a recent letter to IDCO, the Korean company has asked for an item-wise expenditure receipt for the Rs 30.34 crore it had paid towards land acquisition. POSCO followed it up with another letter asking for a refund of Rs 11.21 crore out of the Rs 13.52 crore it had paid towards acquisition of 438 acres of private land for the project, which was never acquired due to stiff opposition from the people of Dhinkia village, the epicentre of the movement against POSCO.

These instances cited here are tips of the iceberg. People's protests against displacement are widespread all over the state and gaining momentum against the industrial houses. The displaced people of the Mahanadi Coalfields Limited (MCL), a subsidiary of the Coal India have been strongly pressing their demands for rehabilitation, taking resort to agitational methods. Besides, recently protests and agitations are also rising against the proposed coastal ports at different places of Kendrapara, Jagatsinghpur, Balasore, Bhadrak, Puri and Ganjam districts of Odisha. While the state government looks upon all these resistance movements as law and order problems, and has been trying to tighten the security arrangements in and around the industrial hub, the people have raised motley of questions which merit serious attention of the corporate bodies. Besides the questions of rehabilitation and resettlement, the questions of betterment of the quality of life of the project-affected people, an important segment of the stakeholders, are intimately associated with all these movements. More over globalisation has brought in economic patriotism, a new force that is very much active.

As observed here all these protest movements are mainly directed against displacement of people and for protection of the local environment. The people complain against poor rate of compensation and gross inadequacies in matters of resettlement and rehabilitation. There are several instances in the past in which people have suffered heavily due to apathy of the state government wherever major projects were undertaken. As regards employment benefits to the displaced people, it is found that the PSUs have been lagging far behind in the state. It is estimated that the MCL is yet to provide jobs to nearly 2,017 displaced families and, the Neelachal Ispat Nigam at Kalinga Nagar to at least 450 in recent years.

Over a period of five decades the Rourkela Steel Plant has not solved this problem for which the people are agitating. Mostly, the people who are hit very hard in the process are the poor farmers, the tribals and other people of the weaker sections of the society. The government bureaucracy is not responsive to the needs of the displaced people and people's discontentment against industrialisation find expression through various methods which have serious social, economic and political implications.

As regards industrialisation of Odisha in the present context, many questions have been raised. We are yet to find out satisfactory answers to them. The first and foremost of them relates to total depletion of mineral deposits. The state has 5,428 million tones of iron ore deposits of which the government can recommend mining lease for 1,529 million tones. The rest has already been leased out to various companies. If all the 43 projects start working, they will need 2,785 million tones of ore creating a shortfall of 1,256 million tones. The mega POSCO plant alone needs 600 million tonnes.

The second question relates to acute shortage of water for the purpose of irrigation. Widespread mining activities would certainly lead to drying up of the natural sources of water. It is estimated that nearly one crore of agriculturists would be affected by industrialisation. All the rivers, springs and other sources of water are getting dry up in view of mining activities in Koraput, Keonjhar, and Sundargarh districts recently. The mega industrial units would require water which now feeds the paddy fields of the state. The cultivators of Sambalpur have been raising their voice against supply of water from the reservoir of the Hirakud Dam to the industrial units located in and around Sambalpur and Jharsuguda. Unless proper care is taken, industrialisation may have a great adverse impact on agriculture and ruin the economy of the villages.

In this context, we may refer to the report of the World Bank on India. It has been mentioned in the report that 43 per cent of the rural population in Odisha is very poor due to fall in agricultural production which has a damaging impact on rural economy. The report makes it clear that there is a declining trend in agricultural production. While the growth rate during 1980 to 1992 was 3.2 per cent, it came down to 2.4 per cent during 1992 to 2003. Thirdly, it may be pointed out that the average life span of a plant is 35 to 50 years. Widespread mining operations are sure to result in destruction of forests and green belts. The devoured land mass may not be suitable for agriculture nor for any productive purpose. People in Africa, Australia and in other places have paid a heavy price for unregulated industrialisation.

The fourth question relates to economic patriotism. Globalisation has opened the doors for all multi-national entrepreneurs. All business houses run for profit. Industrialisation through foreign investors inducing displacement of local people may be an issue with which people may not reconcile easily. The rehabilitation and resettlement policy needs to be formulated in such a way that the people feel that they are not the losers. The offer needs to be made attractive and make the people willing to accept it. Attachment to hearths and homes, community assets and local resources forms a natural bond among the people in a locality. It is a social reality which is woven with the threads of the psycho-social behaviour of the individual and community in a locality for a number of generations. In all matters of development induced mass displacement State intervention may be desirable with utmost care. In a competitive system, the party in power takes the decision on behalf of the government. The opposition may look for an opportunity for political mobilisation on an issue to discredit the government. The bureaucracy has its own way to implement government decisions.

To what extent structural adjustment has been made following liberalisation and globalisation since 1991 to suit the present condition is a big question. It is the people who are called upon to make the sacrifice. The situation needs a thorough analysis and great understanding by the policy-makers. Whether we live in an age of nationalism or globalisation it is the people who matter. Instead of going deep into the real grievances of the project affected people, the party in power as well as the opposition groups is busy in rallying the people in their favour, creating factions and cleavages at the grass-roots. The real issues of human dignity are lost in the ongoing political controversies. The most important issues which have surface the movements are livelihood issues and rights of the certain sections people which include the tribals, peasants and the fisher folk for whom the compensation package and rehabilitation measures hold out no promise.

Orissa Resettlement and Rehabilitation Policy - 2006

The bloody episode of 2nd January 2006, that killed twelve tribals and one police man at Kalinga Nagar made a sudden spurt of an unprecedented rage against displacement in general and displacement of tribals in particular. The episode rocked not only Odisha but sent tremors across the adjacent tribal populated States like Chhattishgarh and Jharkhand, which was so to say the single greatest compulsion behind the Government of Odisha to go for an immediate proclamation of a comprehensive, eye-catching R&R policy in a bid to defuse the explosive anger of the public at large. Though the discussion around the need for a comprehensive R&R Policy for the State as a whole was afoot for a long time, it was the bloody episode of Kalinganagar killings on 2nd January 2006 that hastened the process at the official level for its prompt finalisation and eventual notification on the extraordinary gazette of Orissa dated 15th May 2006. Soon after the Kalinganagar episode, the State Government constituted a Group of Ministers under the Chairmanship of Sri Biswabhushan Harichandan, the then Minister for Law and Industry, Odisha to finalise the draft of a comprehensive State policy for R&R as quickly as possible. An 'information sheet' mentioning the past efforts made in respect of

R&R policy in the State was brought out by the Government for appraisal of the said Group on the occasion of their first meeting held on 28th January, 2006. From the said information sheet one can reconstruct a trajectory of piecemeal project-related and sector-related packages for compensation and benefits evolving finally into a comprehensive State level policy for resettlement and rehabilitation for project displaced families.

Mining sector policy came into vogue in 1989 with the introduction of R&R Policy for Mahanadi Coalfields Limited. The policy for the water resources sector that came into force in 1994 marks an important stage in the evolution of resettlement policies from project specific to sector specific policies. The following were the three major Orissa State Sectoral Policies, covering projects in water resources, industries and mining sectors.

- Resettlement and Rehabilitation Policy for one of the largest Public Sector Undertakings in the Country and operating in Orissa, NALCO was framed in the year 1984.
- In the mining sector, uniform guidelines for rehabilitation of the displaced persons/families due to SECL (South Eastern Coalfield Ltd.), presently Mahanadi Coalfields Limited, 1989, popularly known as R&R Policy of MCL, 1989.
- R&R policies have been made for Interim Test Range, Chandipur in the district of Balasore, 1993.
- The Orissa Resettlement and Rehabilitation of Project Affected Persons Policy (Water Resources), 1994.
- Guidelines for Rehabilitation of Displaced Persons/Families in connection with establishment of Steel Plant of Tata Steel at Gopalpur in Ganjam District, 1996.
- R&R policies for Kalinganagar Integrated Industrial Complex at Duburi in the district of Jajpur was framed in the year 1997.

- Policy for Rehabilitation of Displaced Persons/Families in connection with establishment of Major Industrial Projects, 1998.
- Policy for Rehabilitation of Displaced Persons/Families in case of Mining Projects, 1998.
- Aditya Alumunium Project Resettlement and Rehabilitation of Project Affected Persons Policy, 1999.
- R&R policies have been made for Utkal Alumina and Vedanta Alumina in the districts of Rayagada and Kalahandi respectively in the year 2003.
- Revised R&R policies for Kalinganagar Integrated Industrial Complex, Duburi in the district of Jajpur in November, 2005.

(*Source:* Information Sheet for the Meeting of Group of Ministers held on 28.01.2006)

Basic Objectives

In order to ensure sustained development through a participatory and transparent process, Government of Odisha framed a comprehensive resettlement and rehabilitation policy. Basic objectives of the policy are:-

- to avoid displacement wherever possible and minimise it exercising available options otherwise.
- to ensure environmental sustainability through participatory and transparent process.
- to recognise voices of displaced communities emphasising the needs of the indigenous communities and vulnerable sections.
- to help guiding the process of developing institutional mechanism for implementation, monitoring, conflict resolution and grievance redressal.

Project Types

For the purpose of R&R benefits under this Policy, Development Projects are classified into the following types. (See Figure 3.1)

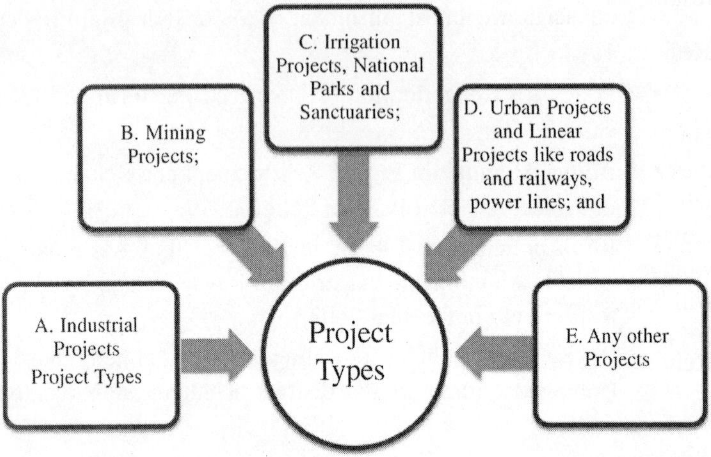

Figure 3.1: Project Types

A. Industrial Projects;

B. Mining Projects;

C. Irrigation Projects, National Parks and Sanctuaries;

D. Urban Projects and Linear Projects like roads and railways, power lines; and

E. Any other Projects

Land Acquisition and Payment of Compensation/Award

Procedure prescribed by Government shall be followed in acquiring land and other property and for payment of compensation award. All compensation money due to the displaced families shall be paid through account payee cheques. As regards public property like School Building, Club House, Hospital, Panchayat Ghar, electrical installation, place(s) of worship, value of such property affected shall be deposited with the concerned District Collector. Either Project or District Administration shall take up construction at the place as would be determined in consultation with representatives of displaced persons. The Project proponent may opt for direct purchase of land on the basis of negotiated price after issue of notification requiring acquisition of land under relevant Act(s). If acquisition of land through direct purchase fails, other provisions of the relevant Act may be invoked. Land not utilised by the Project within the prescribed time limit and for the required purposes shall be resumed.

Resettlement and Rehabilitation Plan

Based on the list approved by Government and option of displaced families, Resettlement and Rehabilitation Plan shall be prepared by the Collector for resettlement and rehabilitation after due consultation with displaced communities in the manner determined by the Government. Such plan should address the specific needs of the women, vulnerable groups and indigenous communities. The same will be placed before the RPDAC for approval.

Rehabilitation Assistance

Rehabilitation Assistance will be specific to the type of project as mentioned above, because of difference in nature of projects, their source (s) of funding and magnitude of displacement;[1] impact. Here the benefits to the DPs in case of Industrial Projects are discussed.

(a) Employment: Families shall be eligible for employment, by the project causing displacement or loss of all agricultural land. For the purpose of employment, each original family will nominate one member of such family. The project proponent will give preference to the nominated members of the displaced /other families in the matter of employment. The order of preference will be as follows:

1. Displaced families losing all land including homestead land,
2. Displaced families losing more than 2/3rd of agricultural land and homestead land,
3. Displaced families losing more than 1/3rd of agricultural land and homestead land,
4. Displaced families losing only homestead land but not agricultural land,
5. Families losing all agricultural land but not homestead land.

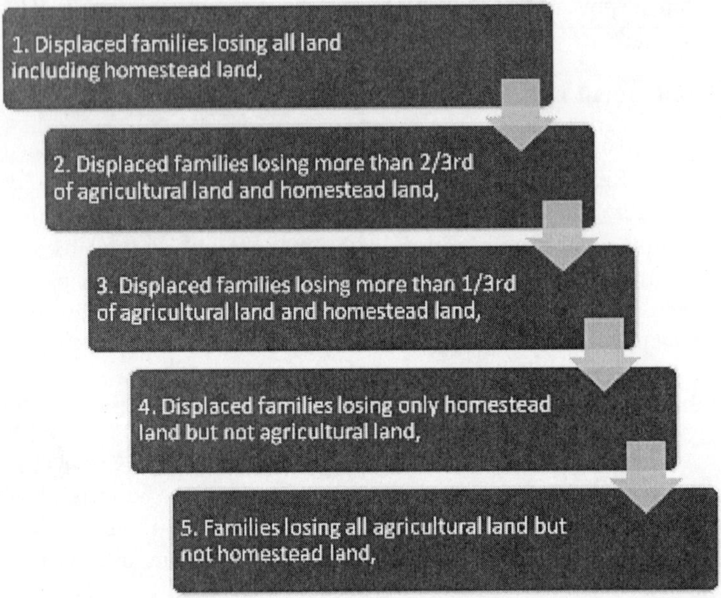

Figure 3.2: The order of preference

The Project authority will make special efforts to facilitate skill up-gradation of the nominated member of each displaced/other family to make him/her employable in their project. Displaced/other families who are eligible to be considered for employment and families defined under clause 1 to 5 shall be provided with one time cash assistance in lieu of employment/self-employment in the scale indicated below:

Sl. No.	*Families under category*	*Amount of onetime Cash assistance (As per new revision on 28.07.2014)*
1.	Displaced families coming under category 1	Rs 8,50,000.00
2.	Displaced families coming under category 2	Rs 5,10,000.00
3.	Displaced families coming under category 3	Rs 3,40,000.00
4.	Displaced families coming under category 4 & 5	Rs 1,70,000.00

(b) Training for Self-employment: Project authority under the guidance of the District Collector will make adequate arrangement to provide vocational training to at least one member of each displaced other family so as to equip him/her to start his/her own small enterprise and refine his/her skills to take advantage of new lob opportunities. For those engaged in traditional occupations/handicrafts/handlooms, suitable training shall be organised at the cost of project authority to upgrade their existing skills.

(c) Convertible Preference Share: At the option of the displaced family and, subject to the provisions of relevant law(s) in force for the time being, the project authority may issue Convertible Preference Share(s) or Secured Bond(s) up to a maximum of 50 per cent out of one time cash assistance.

(d) Provision for homestead land: Subject to availability, each displaced family will be given at least 1/10th of an acre of land free of cost in a resettlement habitat for homestead purpose.

(e) Assistance for Self-relocation: Each of the displaced family who opts for self-relocation elsewhere other than the Resettlement habitat shall be given a onetime cash grant of Rs 85,000 (As per new revision on 28.07.2014) in lieu of homestead land.

(f) House Building Assistance: Besides, Project authority shall construct house for each of the displaced families in the resettlement habitat or provide house building assistance of Rs 2,55,000 (As per new revision on 28.07.2014) to each of the displaced families settling in the Resettlement habitat or opting for self relocation elsewhere.

(g) Shops and Service Units: Project authorities will also construct shops and service units at feasible locations at their own cost, which will be allotted in consultation with Collector to project displaced families opting for self-employment. While allotting such units, preference will be given to physically challenged persons and members of displaced SC & ST families.

Benefit to landless & homestead-less encroachers common to all categories

(a) An encroacher family, who is landless as defined in the Orissa Prevention of Land Encroachment Act, 1972, and is in possession of the encroached land at least for a period of ten years continuously prior to the date of notification under relevant law(s) declaring intention of land acquisition will get ex-gratia equal to compensation admissible under the Land Acquisition Act, 1894 for a similar category of land to the extent of land under his/her physical possession up to a maximum of one standard acre, if the encroachment is unobjectionable. While determining the extent of land for such compensation the rayati land held by him/her is to be taken into account.

(b) An encroacher family, who is homestead less as defined in the Orissa Prevention of Land Encroachment Act, 1972 and is in possession of the encroached land at least for a period of ten years continuously prior to the date of notification under relevant law(s) declaring intention of land acquisition will get ex-gratia, equal to compensation for the similar category of homestead land, against the encroached homestead land up to a maximum of 1/l0th of an acre in rural areas or 1/25th of an acre in urban areas, if the encroachment is unobjectionable. While determining the extent of land for such compensation the homestead land held by him/her is to be taken into account. The ex-gratia will be in addition to the actual cost of structures thereon. If the encroachment is found to be objectionable, (s)he will be entitled to the cost of structure only.

Other Assistance : Common to all categories of projects

(a) Maintenance Allowance: In order to ensure timely vacation, an allowance of Rs 3,400 per month per displaced family shall be provided on vacation of land/house for a period of one year from the date of vacation as determined by the Collector concerned.

(b) Assistance for Temporary Shed: An assistance of Rs 17,000 shall be provided to each displaced family.

(c) Transportation Allowance: Transportation allowance of Rs 3,400 or free transportation to the resettlement habitat or their new place of inhabitance, shall be provided to each displaced family by the Project Authority.

Special benefits to displaced indigenous families and primitive tribal groups.

(a) While developing the resettlement plans, the socio-cultural norms of indigenous and primitive tribal groups will be respected.

(b) Each displaced family of indigenous category shall be given preferential allotment of land.

(c) As far as practicable, indigenous communities should be resettled in a compact area close to their natural habitat.

(d) Indigenous displaced families resettled outside the district shall be given 25 per cent higher R&R benefits in monetary terms.

Periphery Development

The Project authorities shall be responsible for periphery development as decided by the RPDAC within the guidelines issued from time to time by the State Government.

Compensation Advisory Committee

Government in Revenue Department may constitute a District Compensation Advisory Committee (DCAC) under the chairmanship of the Collector to determine negotiated price. Adequate representation will be given to women and indigenous communities (wherever applicable) in the committee. If any dispute arises on recommendation of the DCAC, the matter will be referred to the State level Compensation Advisory Committee (SCAC) chaired by the Member-Board of Revenue whose decisions shall be final and binding on all concerned. The composition of this State level Compensation Advisory Committee will be notified by the Government.

Rehabilitation and Periphery Development Advisory Committee (RPDAC)

In order to encourage participation of displaced people and their elected representatives in implementation and monitoring of R&R package, to oversee and monitor periphery development the Govt.

may constitute a Rehabilitation-cum-Periphery Development Advisory Committee (RPDAC) for each or a group of projects falling in one district, The detailed composition of the Committee shall be notified by the Government and it may include peoples representatives, one or two leading NGOs of the affected area and select Government officers, and any other persons to be notified by the Government, Adequate representation will be given to women and indigenous communities (wherever applicable) in the committee. Chairman of the committee will be at liberty to co-opt members for efficient discharge of its functions.

State Level Council on Resettlement and Rehabilitation (SLCRR)

At the State level, there will be a Council headed by the Chief Minister to advise, review and monitor implementation of Resettlement and Rehabilitation Policy. The Council may comprise of Ministers, select representatives of the people, leading social activists, academicians and experts of national and international repute and senior officials of the Government.

Grievance Redressal Mechanism

An effective Grievance Redressal Mechanism will be set up at District and Directorate level to deal with grievance of the project displaced people relating to land acquisition, resettlement and rehabilitation. Besides, all the project authorities shall be asked to set up an effective Grievance Redressal Mechanism relating to their project. Effective participation of the displaced communities will be ensured in the process.

Notes

1. Fernandes, W. (2004) *Rehabilitation Policy for the Displaced.*
2. Dalua, A.K. (1991), *"Irrigation in Odisha". A Compilation by Irrigation Department,* Government of Orissa, Bhubaneswar.
3. Baboo, Balgovind (1992), *"Technology and Social Transformation- The Case of the Hirakud Multipurpose Dam Project in Odisha",* Concept Publishing Company, New Delhi.
4. Dhagamwar and et. al (2003) *Industrial Development and Displacement, The People of Korba,* Sage Publication, New Delhi.

5. Dharmadhikari et. al. (2005), *Unraveling BHAKRA*, Manthan Adhyaayan Kendra, Badwani.
6. Fernandes, W. (2004), *Rehabilitation Policy for the Displaced,*
7. Downing, T.(2005) *Rights for the World's Evicted: Are Development Projects*
8. Cernea, M. (1999) (Ed), *The Economics of Involuntary Resettlement: Questions and Challenges,* World Bank Washington, D.C.
9. Dhritri (2012) *Diversion of Forest Land for Mining, Industries etc.* Odiya Daily, 9th Jan.

Chapter 4

Challenges

India has been undertaking development projects to improve the quality of life of its people through planned development under the successive Five-Year Plans since its independence in 1947. Such projects include dams, power, mining, industrial and allied infrastructures, transport network, urban development, commercial forestry and other projects. Some of these projects have brought adverse effects in the form of displacement of people from their original place of habitation due to large-scale land acquisition. Development-induced displacement in the country has brought severe economic, social and environmental problems to the displaced people. Magnitude of people displaced and severity of the problems due to multipurpose dam projects is too high as compared to other projects in the country. They also lead to submergence of high quality of land, destruction of the watershed, disturb the delicate ecological balance and distort the surrounding environment, loss of wildlife and precious irreplaceable flora, etc. and most notorious problems of flooding, water-logging and salinity. The experience of post-Independence period from projects across the country suggests that the long drawn out process of displacement has caused widespread traumatic psychological and socio-cultural consequences. These include the dismantling of traditional production systems, violation of ancestral sacred zones, graves and places of worship, scattering of kinship groups, disruptions of family system and informal social network Michael M. Cernea (1997)[1] has developed the .risk and reconstruction model, which has already been tested to be applicable to the development induced displacement situation in the country. The model is built around a core concept: the risks of impoverishment. The eight-impoverishment risks are landlessness, joblessness, homelessness, marginalisation, food insecurity, increased morbidity and mortality, loss of access to common property and social disarticulation. Mega development projects like construction of dams, industries, highways and roads resulted in forced displacement of the people. It has been found that usually it is the poor people who face the consequences of such projects more because their livelihood, habitat and assets are affected. Where "involuntary resettlement" has received public attention, either through NGOs or media intervention, the state administration has responded. In most of the cases such displacements have resulted in loss of livelihood and shelter.

Following are some examples in which NHRC received complains and expressed its concern in cases of displacement as a result of development projects.

(i) Bargi Dam oustees in Madhya Pradesh

(ii) Kabini Reservoir Project, Karnataka

(iii) Bandipur National Park- Project Tiger

The Special Economic Zone Act, 2005 has been passed with a view to promote foreign investment, export oriented growth and the need for a level playing field for domestic enterprises and manufacturers so as to be competitive globally. Several civil society groups, activists and organisations have expressed the fear that this process could lead to acquisition of agricultural land causing large scale displacement of farmers in the name of industrialisation. Hence, there is a need to provide suitable relief and rehabilitation package, including giving stakes to the displaced persons whose land has been acquired for setting up of SEZs. In the state of West Bengal, large scale violence took place in March and November 2007 on the issue of proposed land acquisition for setting up a mega chemical hub and a Special Economic Zone covering about 10,000 acres of land in Nandigram and adjoining areas. The commission took cognizance of the case and not only called for report from the State Government but also sent its own investigation team.

Development caused displacement generates varied responses from different sections of society and it also creates a differential impact on the lives of people. It is generally believed that development efforts, which does not leave majority of its people worse off and promotes health, education and income could be regarded as participatory. But most of the development projects operate in totally opposite direction where majority of the project affected families are left to fend for themselves with poorly planned, badly executed, inappropriate and inadequate rehabilitation plans. The resettlement and rehabilitation for them becomes all the more difficult in the absence of state level policy and legislative mechanisms. This is the case of India where compulsory acquisition of land for public purpose particularly for infrastructural and industrial projects in public and private sector has aggravated the already existing inequalities and is instrumental in uprooting people from their natural habitats both in the pre and post-independence periods. With globalisation and trade liberalisation, the increased demand for land has provided further boost to the miseries of displaced persons evicting them from their homes and forcing them to give away their assets and means of livelihood. Women are the worst affected among the displaced people. Being the most discriminated and vulnerable, displacements add to their already existing miseries. Development process thus has brought forward the biggest challenge of resettlement and rehabilitation of the persons displaced by the development projects.

Land Acquisition in India is done under the Land Acquisition Act (LAA), 1894. This Act does not have any provision for rehabilitation. Since then until 1985, any state government or Central Government enacted no legislation or a policy for resettlement and rehabilitation. It was only when states like Madhya Pradesh in 1985, Karnataka in 1987 and Maharashtra in 1989 enacted laws however, without properly laid down rules and regulations for resettlement and rehabilitation of the people displaced from state-level water resource projects; the legacy of the colonial government was broken. Public sector companies like National Thermal Power Corporation (NTPC) and Coal India Limited (CIL) also came out with their policies in 1993 and 1994 respectively. These policies were, however, alleged to be formulated under the pressure from the World Bank. Government of India has come out with a National Policy on Resettlement and Rehabilitation (NPRR) for Project Affected Families, 2003, which was published in the Gazette of India on February 17, 2004. The first draft of this policy was brought out in1993 and thus the policy was long overdue. This policy has however generated a debate among the scholars about its relevance for the project-displaced people. Some scholars compared this policy document with proposed draft of the policy and came out with the observations that the policy is regressive in its nature. Others viewed it an election stunt of the previous government. Comparing it with the old Land Acquisition Act (LAA), 1894 the researchers find that both NPRR and LAA have conflicting clauses and that the former serves the vested interests of the land requiring body. However when it comes to neglecting the vulnerable sections of society including women, the NPRR follows the spirit of the LAA. The policy is also viewed as a package with a series of barriers, assumptions and conditions, which while criticising cash compensation, actually bases itself on cash instruments and serves the agenda of corporate globalisation. Displacement is described as dislocation of people from their native place and region. It often exacerbates rather than mitigates economic insecurity, helplessness and alienation. This could mean loss of economic livelihoods and communities. After independence the developmental projects were launched by the government, which were formulated, designed and carried out by the engineers and bureaucrats, who had no concern for environmental and rehabilitation issues. There is a disagreement over exact number of displaced people. Various studies on displacement point out that in earlier phase until 1980 was marked by meagre compensation towards the affected people and lack of any attempt to understand the issues of rehabilitation of the displaced people. Most of the affected people were from poor households and with the displacement they were further marginalised due to loss of their livelihoods. The involuntary displacement of people due to acquisition of their land for developmental activities across India is a major issue. They have resulted in widespread protests across the country. People began to protests, for example, major projects such as Sardar Sarovar, Salient Valley, the Manglore Thermal Power, the Dabhol power, Maha Mumbai Special Economic Zones, the Nandigram SEZ, the Singur Tata Motors.

Impact of Displacement

In India there has been large number of protest rising against the compulsory acquisition of land by the government or its agencies, for example acquisition of land for POSCO in Jagatsinghpur, TATA in Kalinga Nagar, for the manufacture of Tata Nano in Singur, land acquisition for developing SEZ in Nandigram etc. In most of the case it has been seen that it is the agricultural land which is acquired by the government/government agency. The impact of displacement takes various forms such as economic and social, cultural and political, psychological and environmental. The fallouts of development-induced displacement can also be seen in the economic sphere. The problems faced by the displaced people are landlessness and disruptive change in the land- holding pattern. Thus the main reason for protest against the compulsory land acquisition is the forced acquisition of this agricultural land, for which the protestor thinks that they have not been properly paid. Some of the potential risks which are associated with the forced displacement are:

Loss of Land

Loss of land and change in the land-holding pattern is one of the principal forms of dispossession that results from rural displacement. Expropriation of land removes the main foundation upon which people's productive systems, commercial activities and livelihoods are constructed. In other words, loss of land results in people losing their agricultural and homestead land that provides food and economic security to a large number of people in India. If these livelihood systems are not rebuilt elsewhere or replaced with steady income generating employment then landlessness sets in leading to impoverishment. The various types of people, social groups and villages experience the risk of landlessness differently. It is the agricultural land which is mostly acquired by the appropriate government/government agencies. Thus, with the forced displacement the people may lose the land which was their sole mode of livelihood.

Homelessness

The losses of the shelter in some cases are temporary, as they may be resettled in some other place. But it not true with all the affected persons and most of them are forced to remain homeless for the large period of time. Homelessness is another form of economic dispossession. Though the loss of housing and shelter is temporary for most displaced persons, this phase can be very long and traumatic by nature. There an example of the problem of homelessness. In the early 1970s, no provision of construction of housing for displaced people was made by the Project authorities. Instead, those displaced were provided with homestead plots on which the people were expected to build their own houses. This created a state of homelessness of the displaced people such as in the case of Bharat Heavy Electricals Limited (BHEL) in Andhra Pradesh and the Bokaro Steel Plant in Jharkhand etc. Interviews conducted by Muhammad Asif with the oustees of the Bokaro Steel Plant for his study on *Development-Induced Displacement in Jharkhand'* (Asif 1997) speaks volumes of the harrowing experiences that the people went through as a result of homelessness. In this case, the oustees were brought from their original place and dumped on an open ground-with not even a temporary roof over their heads. The displaced people remained in this state of homelessness for two to three years, and had to make do with tents during the period. Through sheer negligence, the Project authorities had not made provision for enough homestead plots for all the oustees. As a result there was a mad rush among them to find a place in the resettlement colony. Those who reached the place first found a plot. The rest were rendered homeless[2]. At some of the resettlement sites of Sardar Sarovar Dam like Kharagda, Vyavyara, Chinddiapur and Sandia, people used whatever salvaged material they could carry from their origin place to build their houses. Although the R&R process supported the dismantling and transportation of the material, some of the building material was damaged during transportation and consequently the new houses were of poor quality. The walls of the houses were not strong because the bamboo, with which the houses were generally built, was damaged during transportation was not available in the new site. Consequently, over time, the oustees at Tentalav and Sukka were able to construct only semi-pucca houses, which were not suitable for the monsoons in the area. Before submergence, their houses were built on hillsides where rainwater did not collect because of the natural drainage on the slopes. Now, the DPs & PAPs complained that because they could not afford to build concrete floors, the rainwater, which collected inside their houses, created tremendous problems for them[3] .

Loss of Job

The service which the native people had in any enterprise or other place is lost. But this loss of job can be replaced by the opportunity of work which the native people will get after the establishment of the industry. After all one of the objective of adopting SEZ in India is that it creates job opportunity.

Loss of access to Common Property

The common property such as wells, gazing lands which is attached with the acquired land is also lost. Other risks which are inherent in displacement are food insecurity, moralisation, loss of schooling of the children etc.

Loss of Livelihood and Impoverishment

Impoverishment is a process of decline in the economic position of the oustees due to loss of basic sources of livelihood. Landlessness, joblessness and homelessness are all indications of this process of marginalisation. It is an indication that the loss of land, the loss of productive assets, and the loss of livelihood have resulted in downward mobility. It occurs when families cannot fully restore their lost economic strength. In this process, middle income farm households do not become landless, but become small holders. Families that were earlier precariously balanced above the poverty line fall blow it and never recover totally even though they may not become landless. In the case of farming families, partial but significant loss of family land to roads or canal may make some farms economically non-viable. High productivity farmers on fertile soil, although they may be given some land, also may face the risk of economic non-viability.

Absence of Food Security

Food insecurity is caused by loss of land, livelihood and access to non-timber produce. Because of displacement, there is a drop in food production and loss of harvests, especially during the transfer from the old to the new site. In addition, rebuilding food production capacity at the relocation site may take years. These losses affect food production, availability of food and the pattern of food consumption. It results in food insecurity, which is defined as intake levels of calories of protein far below the minimum necessary for normal growth and work. Food insecurity worsens particularly during the pre-monsoon period when food intake levels are rather low among the landless, and when resettlement normally takes place. Displacement also leads to changes in dietary intake in the household and that may adversely affect the nutrition level, more specifically of children and women.

Social Disorganisation

Social disorganisation takes place with the type of changes that are brought about by the displacement process. These forces lead to major changes in the social structure of the communities in general and especially of tribal societies. Their family life may be disrupted. The traditional social control mechanisms may be weakened and even lost. Consequently, social tensions may increase. Also social support networks tend to disintegrate and that has far reaching consequences for the community. Social networks often heip people cope with poverty through personalised strategies such as informal loans, exchange of food, clothing, durable goods, mutual help with farming, building houses and caring for children. Loss of such multifunctional, yet virtually invisible social networks through displacement acts as a hidden but serious cause of impoverishment through displacement.

Loss of Self-esteem and Identity

Often the development Project oustees experience loss of self-esteem as individuals and as communities, when confronted with development and modernisation. The loss of the moral worth and dignity of a village community can be substantial and as well as socially crippling.

Loss of Culture and Religion

Due to displacement, the oustees also face the risk of losing their culture and religious practices. They lose their cultural autonomy and in the process, their very identity is put at stake. Consequently, every area of their life from language to marriage customs and religion comes under attack. There is gradual collapse of the religious ethos that is closely linked to their environment and socio-agrarian systems. The community festivals, which held tremendous importance in the lives of the people, lose their meaning.

Loss of Political Institutions

In the political sphere, dispossession takes place through the process of political integration in the so-called national polity. This gradually leads to the traditional political systems and institutions' redundancy. The displaced people are incorporated into the state and have to conform to and become integrated with the so-called mainstream political system.

Psychological Impact

Research has shown that displacement and dislocation causes special cultural, economic and technical problems. Studies have shown that a feeling of alienation, helplessness and powerlessness is instilled in those uprooted. Social cohesion is weakened and increased psychological stress diminishes the initiative and capacity for collective action of those affected. Displacement may also lead .to social anomie and emotional disorders.

Loss of Health

Displacement adversely affects the health status of the community, which is a sensitive· indicator of development. It has also been seen that people forced to relocate have a higher degree of exposure to illness and to comparatively more severe illness, than those who are not. Adverse health effects of displacement result particularly when projects do not incorporate preventive epidemiological measures. The direct and secondary effects of involuntary dislocation without preventive health measures rank from diseases of poor hygiene, such as diarrhea and dysentery, to outbreaks of parasitic and vector-borne diseases such as malaria and schistosomiasis caused by unsafe, insufficient water supplies· and inadequate sanitary waste systems.

Impact on Women

A review of the laws and policies dealing with rehabilitation of displaced people reveals that women's concerns and needs are grossly ignored in these policies. LAA, 1894 determines compensation and rehabilitation benefits in the form of cash to displaced people on the basis of the ownership on the land acquired. It recognises only individual and no collective rights. Thus, people depending upon common property resources for generations are not entitled to any compensation under this Act. The Act therefore reflects gender discrimination. It merely reinforces the existing reality of women's lack of ownership and property. Moreover, the cash compensation awarded to the male member of the family has an adverse impact on women as they have no control over the cash compensation. The policies adopted by NTPC and CIL are also considered to have gender discrimination as none of the policies adopted by these public sector undertakings recognise women as independent entity for R&R benefits. CIL policy, however does make a passing reference to the fact that special attempt will be made to ensure that women get adequate access to income generating opportunities offered under R&R policy which provides such benefits only based on the land ownership. So the policy conflicts itself with the existing realities of women owning the land. At the State level, Uttar Pradesh and Madhya Pradesh policies have elements of gender discrimination. Government of Odisha offers a policy with some gender components. In its resolution number 25101, dated 14th July 1992, the policy accorded divorcees (with or without dependent children) and with no source of livelihood; status of a separate family for R&R benefits. The ground reality is however that the required clause for claiming the benefits by submitting an affidavit proving herself to be a divorcee followed by an enquiry of that claim by the office-in-charge; makes it really difficult for such women to avail R&R benefits under the policy. In majority of the cases, the husbands desert these women without a formal divorce. Thus, such clauses make these illiterate women all the more vulnerable as they are at the mercy of the office-in-charge and also it is very difficult for them to get affidavits. At project level, the planners of the Sardar Sarovar Project of Maharashtra Government considered major unmarried daughters for the purpose of R&R. Gujarat government categorically left out unmarried daughters and includes all women widowed after 1980 as separate family for the purpose of R&R benefits. Women widowed prior to 1980 are, however, considered as dependents on the male head of their families. Madhya Pradesh Government, on the other hand, does not mention women at all for resettlement and rehabilitation. The recently adopted National policy on Resettlement and Rehabilitation (NPRR) again shows the same kind of gender discrimination. Thus, the single male adults are able to claim the benefits separately but unmarried women do not receive any benefits and are treated as dependents on their male relative. However, it recognises the concept of family for the purpose of resettlement and rehabilitation where unmarried daughters and unmarried sisters are included. The discernible impacts are given in the figure 4.1.

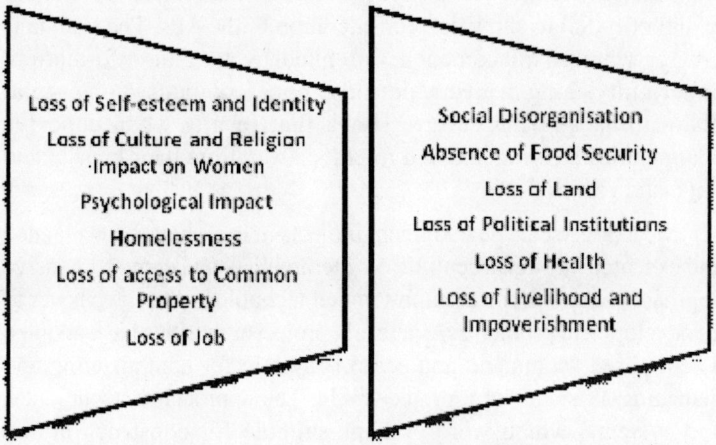

Figure 4.1: Impacts of displacement

Displacement due to Development Projects

The major sectors in which infrastructure projects are implemented in India include irrigation, mining, industry, power, ports, water supply, and roads and highways. Infrastructure projects in these sectors entail acquisition of private land, which requires not only paying compensation to owners but also resettlement and rehabilitation (R&R) of affected persons (APs). Although these projects are important for national development, they often adversely affect some groups. Hence, sound policies and measures needed to protect the lives, human rights, and welfare of such people become an integral part of development projects. Involuntary resettlement will remain a major challenge in the foreseeable future. The number of projects that involve land acquisition will increase. Land is a basic requirement for these projects and owing to rapid population growth uninhabited areas are increasingly becoming scarce. In the circumstances, the only option is to acquire private land in populated areas. People displaced by development projects often have to move elsewhere to start a new life. There is a strong element of compulsion in displacement: long established social networks are disrupted and with them the social systems through which members of the community are sustained. For those forced to resettle in new locations, displacement is indeed an unmitigated disaster. Things become further intolerable when those in authority fail to show due consideration to the APs. The trauma is greater when displacement is attended by lack of information, uncertainty, long waiting periods, poor compensation, social dislocation, and the culture shock that results when cohesive communities are scattered and resettled away from their kinship and linguistic groups.

Most large-scale development projects in India have been planned and executed through a centralised, hierarchical, and capital-intensive approach, based on the assumption that technology has the answer to all development problems. As a result, project authorities have adopted a centralised "command and control" system for administering and managing all stages of a project cycle. The approaches, techniques, and systems, which were perhaps suitable for construction and mechanical production, were applied to communities. Studies point to the impoverishment of APs because of projects and not their state of poverty before the project comes into the area.[4] Article 21 of the Constitution guarantees to every Indian citizen the right to life with dignity. When projects deprive them of their livelihood, they have a right to begin a new life that protects their economic interests, culture, and social system. In national development, policy makers give priority to economic growth rather than to the people. Displaced persons (DPs) are often not resettled satisfactorily. Though externally aided projects have resettlement packages, their approach to resettlement has limitations. Studies show that the strong (high caste, upper-class families, especially men) become stronger. The weak (the poor, low-caste, particularly Women) become weaker.

Effects of Displacement in Odisha

Odisha is rich in mineral resources, but it is poor. Hence, industrialisation of the state is a must to eradicate the poverty, to open up employment opportunities to eradicated and unskilled labour. In the era of liberalisation, privatisation and globalisation, industrialisation is primarily geared towards harnessing the vast natural resources in the state. A large number of mineral processing industries are coming to Odisha to invest in the mineral- rich areas. The adverse effects of these industries are many. It has little scope for employment generation. And it destroys the natural resources and pollutes the environment. Industrialisation including mining activities has received wide acceptance as a major strategy for development all over the world. In the post-independence period, India embarked on a course of industrialisation under the aegis of the public sector, which assumed "commanding heights". The private sector also did not lag far behind under a system called 'mixed economy'.

After a lapse of four decades, there has been a shift in emphasis following the processes of liberalisation, privatisation and globalisation. The strategies, however, continue unchanged though the role of the public sector has been shrinking, assigning an ascending role to the private sector including foreign investors. The corporate houses both private and public are the agencies to carry on directly the programme of industrialisation. However, even in the changed scenario, the state, functioning within a system of competitive politics and democratic framework, continues to be the prime mover and guardian of the whole enterprise. A new trend is in evidence in the process of development in many parts of the country, which poses a serious threat to the process of industrialisation. It not only involves colossal loss and premature closure of the industrial units but also generates a good deal of social tension and political turmoil leading to political instability. While the state taking the advantage of the new economic reforms starts the process of industrialisation, the local people resist the developmental efforts raising a host of questions which affect adversely their lives. In the process the forces which are released create insurmountable difficulties in the path of industrialisation, leading to closure of the units in a few cases. The strategy is put to searching questioning, putting the state in a fix. Odisha is predominantly an agricultural state where nearly seventy per cent of the working population depends on agriculture. The state has nearly forty per cent of Scheduled Castes (SC) and Scheduled Tribes (ST) population, which together make 9.78 million, apart from the people belonging to the Other Backward Castes (OBC). The state is rich in mineral resources. It has 5,428 million tons of iron ore deposit which is one-third of the total iron-ore deposits of the country. One-fourth of the coal deposit of the country is in the state, in addition to 98 to 99 and 63 per cent of chromites and bauxite deposits respectively. Besides, the available infrastructure includes water in plenty, power at a cheap rate, 480 kms of coastline with one large port at Paradip and two proposed ports at Dhamra and Gopalpur.[5] In order to bring about economic development, the government of late has launched a massive programme of industrialisation. In 2005 the state government has signed as many as 43 memoranda of understanding with various corporate bodies for setting up of their industrial units at an investment of Rs 1, 60,000 crore. The state has still certain pockets inhabited by tribal and backward class people which have been identified as industrially least developed areas where the local people are pressing for setting up of industries.[6] It has been estimated that there are as many as 92 industrial units engaged in production of Sponge Iron, which are mainly concentrated in six districts. As regards production of steel, as many as 43 private companies have shown interest to start mining and production. At least eight of them have signed the Memorandum of Understanding (MOU) pending follow up action on their part.

Against this background, the resistance movements of the local people against certain industrial units need to be probed deeply for the future of industrialisation of the state. Voicing protests against industrialisation by the people affected by it is not new in the state but the ongoing movements are different in that they have worked out an unprecedented unity among the tribal and backward masses against the industrial establishments as well as against the state government, making all the major political parties watchful of the situation to derive political mileage. The conflict has caused an impasse. The solution appears to have moved too far.

Notes

1. Michael M.Cernea. *Involuntary Resettlement in Development Projects. Policy Guidelines for Bank- financied Projects.* World Bank Technical Paper Vol. 80. World Bank: Washington, D.C.
2. Fernandes, Walter (et. all) 2001. Development Induced Displacement in Andhra Pradesh, 1951-1995. A Quantitative and Qualitative Study of its Extent and Nature. Indian Social Institute: New Delhi (mimeographed)

3. Singh, Mridula 1992. *Displacement by Sardar Sarovar and Tehri, A Comparative Study of Two Dams.* Multiple Action Research Group: New Delhi.
4. Fernandes, Walter and Mohammed Asif 1997. *Development-Induced Displacement in Orissa, i951 -1995: A Database On Its Extent and Nature.* Indian Social Institute: New Delhi (mimeographed).
5. Districts at a Glance, 2001, Orissa, Directorate of Economics and Statistics, Government of Orissa, 2001; http://www.boloji.com/index.cfm?md= Content&sd=Articles & ArticleID=432#sthash.SxvRq.
6. The people of Baud and Mayurbhanj are demanding for industrialisation Also see Survey of Backward Districts of Orissa (New Delhi; National Council for Applied Economic Research,1969).

   http://www.boloji.com/index.cfm?md=Content&sd=Articles&ArticleID=432#sthash.SxvRqN9H.dpuf

Chapter 5

Rehabilitation Strategies

Resettlement issues focus on the importance of people's participation in selecting appropriate sites for rehabilitation. It examines the viability of either dividing or merging settlements without endangering their socio-cultural integration. Environment Hazard Analysis is an equally important aspect of relocation of DPs. Drawing conclusions from socio-economic survey and study of local infrastructure help in systematising information relating to site selection and preparation of the site. After site selection and its preparation comes the issue of actual movement from previous settlement to the new one after dismantling the old structure and packing all the salvaged material. Transportation of one's belongings is another important aspect of the process. All this is not complete without going through legal formalities. In the absence of a national rehabilitation policy at the Centre, there is no uniformity in the policies adopted by the various state governments for the development projects in their states. Within a state, different departments follow different policies with regard to their respective Projects.

It is a well-known fact that both natural and human made disasters force peo-ple to move out of their land. For example, Tsunami in South Asia in December 2004, Latur and Gujarat earthquake, the Odisha super cyclone and scores of floods and droughts in other parts of our country have rendered thousands of people homeless and jobless. Disasters, like the Bhopal gas tragedy in Union carbide factory, derailment of trains, are examples of human made disaster. Strategies for rehabilitation of thus displaced people are in the first place by way of preventive action. For instance, care is taken to build earthquake proof houses, gather advance information about cyclones and arrange for timely evacuation, build appropriate bunds in flood prone areas, maintain bridges that take regular up and down passing of trains[1] road transport vehicles on them in order to avert likely disasters. Secondly, advance preparation on the part of administration and local communities are made to face the consequences of sudden calamities. For both these remedial steps, the primary necessity is that of building awareness among the people in general and among administrative personnel in particular. The scope for advance planning in the cases of natural and human made calamities is however quite limited and in comparison one can certainly plan better in the cases of development projects which are planned in advance. Development projects come into existence after a fairly long period of planning and awareness of displacement caused by such projects already exists among those who initiate the projects. The tragedy is that despite this prior knowledge of the extent of displacement, those in-charges of development projects pay little attention to the processes of resettlement and rehabilitation of displaced peo-ple. Development projects instead focus on economic efficiency and not on those who stand to lose all that they have, their land, and means of livelihood and stable patterns of social and cultural life. Those who give up substantial portions of their assets for the sake of development projects need to be recognised as stakeholders in development projects. They too need to be a part of develop-ment. The strategies formulated for resettlement and rehabilitation of those displaced by development projects can of course be equally applied to those displaced by natural and human made calamities. As far as our country's preparation for coping with the impact of natural and human made calamities is concerned, we have begun to feel a little aware of negative impacts of such events because they are now occurring at frequent intervals. As a result there are some institutional measure have been taken by the government by way of constituting committees at various levels. They exist on paper and their immediate response to the actual events is yet to come in any significant manner.

Displacement

- Displacement is seen as the result of a model of development that enforces certain technical and economic choices without giving any serious consideration to those options that would involve the least social and environmental costs.

- Most displacement has been involuntary. There has been very little meaningful participation of affected people in the planning and implementation of the dam project, including the resettlement and rehabilitation aspects. The displaced and other affected people have often been the last to receive any meaningful information on the dam project. What information they have received has typically been limited and provided very late in the planning and implementation of mitigation measures.
- The numbers of both directly and indirectly affected people have frequently been underestimated, and there has been an inadequate understanding of the exact nature and extent of the negative effects involved. The State and other project proponents, largely viewing displacement from the standpoint of its causes, consistently maintain that displacement is justified in the larger national interest. It is argued that while some displacement may be inevitable in large development projects, the long term good these projects will bring merits the sacrifice of a few in favour of the larger good. It has stripped displacement of its political content, i.e. the fact that displacement involves the loss of people's rights to land and resources. This has also led to a perception of resettlement and rehabilitation as a reward. Those who view displacement from the point of view of its outcomes would in effect say that though some level of displacement may be inevitable its negative consequences are not.

It is acknowledged that displacement causes severe social, economic, and environmental stresses that translate themselves into physiological, psychological, socio-cultural, economic, and ecological damage. At the same time it is maintained that by expanding resettlement objectives beyond merely aiming to improve the standards of living of the people, it would be possible to offset these disabilities. As a result displacement is largely viewed from the perspective of resettlement and rehabilitation and its attendant complexities. The meaning of displacement has come to be more or less taken for granted, particularly in most academic literature. It is very important to understand that displacement is a multidimensional phenomenon of which physical relocation is only one of the most significant outcomes. The question of displacement is very often reduced to one of effective relocation. At best the displaced are viewed as a group of people who are in need of rehabilitation, not empowerment, for there is no recognition of their disenfranchisement. The displaced people's movements have challenged this view of displacement with physical relocation at its centre and instead have as its core the historical experience of millions of displaced people. This understanding of displacement highlights.

(i) the alienation of the individual and community legal and customary rights and dislocation of the social and economic organisation, and

(ii) the politics of legal and policy instruments that sanctions such disenfranchisement. Displacement refers not only to those who are forced to physically relocate in order to make way for the project and its related aspects but also includes those who are displaced from their resource base and livelihoods. It is commonly experienced through the loss of land and the disruption of social and economic relationships.

Compensation

- Compensation has largely been understood to refer to specific measures intended to make good the losses suffered by people displaced and/or negatively affected by the Project. Compensation usually takes the form of a one-off payment, either in cash or kind and is principally about awards to negatively affected persons.[1]
- The losses incurred by people affected by the creation of infrastructure such as project offices and township, canals, transmission lines, and other activities are not usually properly accounted for and so these losses have not been adequately compensated.
- Compensation is most often awarded only to persons in possession of undisputed legal title. Tenants, sharecroppers, wage-labourers, artisans and encroachers are rarely

considered eligible for compensation, whereas they are paradoxically the most vulnerable and in need of support.

- Community assets and common resources like grasing grounds and forests, which again may be critical for the livelihood of the poorest, are not compensated for under the acquisition process.
- The limited provisions in law to challenge the rate of compensation are, in practice, inaccessible to the negatively affected persons, because they may not be aware of the legal nuances or else cannot afford the expensive remedy of courts. Even those that are able to access courts fritter away a substantial proportion of the gains that they achieve in legal costs.
- Many studies have recorded how cash compensation is depleted by negatively affected persons in short periods, by fraud, for repayment of old debts, in liquor and conspicuous consumption. A lifetime of livelihood security or shelter is squandered in months, sometimes weeks, condemning displaced persons to assured and irrevocable destitution.

Compensation has primarily addressed the loss of assets and property and not rights.

The basis of compensation has thus been

(i) Legal ownership and

(ii) Individual claim.

The general practice is to pay compensation for lost fixed assets like agricultural land at the prevailing market rate, calculated as an average of registered sales prices of land of similar quality and location in the recent past. It is value in exchange rather than value of replacement that is the basis of compensation. To consider a typical example, the Fact-finding Committee on the Srisailam Project found that the replacement value of one acre of dry land was around Rs 5000, and for one acre of wet land Rs 13800. The compensation actually paid was only Rs 932 and Rs 2,332 respectively. In this way, the amount paid as compensation was five times less than the amount that would be required by the negatively affected persons to purchase agricultural land of equivalent quantity and quality. Compensation on basis of replacement value still restricts it to individually owned property; the totality of rights that are violated are not compensated. The most critical of these are:

- The customary rights of people to natural resources that are vital to livelihood and food security;
- The loss of the common property resources which constitute a valuable shared productive base of the community.

This highlights the need for compensation to be relocated in a framework of restitution of rights, both community and individual, beyond even replacement value.

3.3 Resettlement and Rehabilitation

Resettlement programmes have mainly concentrating on the process of physical relocation rather than on the economic and social development of the displaced and other negatively affected people. This has severely eroded the development effectiveness of resettlement and rehabilitation programmes and heightened the impoverishment risk of the resettlers. According to Cernea (1998)[2] risks to adversely affected people are not a component of conventional project analysis. The key economic risks to affected people are from the loss of livelihood and income sources such as arable land, common property resources such as forests, grazing land, ground and surface water, fisheries, etc and changed access to and control of productive resources. The loss of economic power with the breakdown of complex livelihood systems results in temporary or permanent, often irreversible, decline in living standards leading to marginalisation. Higher risks and uncertainties are introduced when diversified livelihood sources are lost. Loss of livelihood and disruption of agricultural activity can adversely affect household food security, leading to under- nourishment. Higher incidence of diseases associated with deteriorating water quality can result in increased morbidity and mortality. High mortality rates, immediately after involuntary resettlement in Kariba and High Aswan dams, are cases in point. As Cernea notes (1998), forced displacement tears apart the existing social fabric, leading to socio-cultural disarticulation.

- Most projects have long planning horizons and the actual physical relocation comes a long time after the initial notifications. The interim period is one full of uncertainties and enormous psycho social anxieties for the to-be-relocated communities. Numerous examples exist of communities being subjected to multiple displacements by successive development projects.

- The costs of the resettlement programme have invariably been underestimated and under-financed. It is often the case that it is always the resettlement and rehabilitation budget that is reduced whenever the project runs into financial problems.
- Institutional weaknesses, marked by confusions between various departments and the lack of capacity as well as continuity, have been major problems in ensuring effective resettlement.
- In the absence of policy and legal instruments and an effective mechanism to monitor compliance, even well-structured institutions with trained staff have failed in consistent implementation of effective resettlement.
- Generally, participation of the affected people has been superficial or treated as unimportant by those responsible for the project. More often they have been manipulated, co-opted, or directly excluded.
- Evidence suggests that for a vast majority of the indigenous/tribal peoples displaced by big projects the experience has been extremely negative in cultural, economic, and health terms. The outcomes have included assetless, unemployment, debt-bondage, hunger, and cultural disintegration. For both indigenous and non-indigenous communities studies, show that displacement has disproportionately impacted on women and children.
- Resettlement sites are invariably selected without reference to availability of livelihood opportunities, or the preferences of displaced persons themselves. Sometimes even temporary shelters are unavailable, and the first few months in the new site are spent in the monsoon rains under the open sky. House-sites are often much smaller than those in which the

resettled people lived in the village, and temporary structures where they exist are made of tin or other inappropriate material and design.

- The question of livelihoods is a major issue in resettlement and rehabilitation policy. There is reluctance on the part of governments and leading agencies to adopt and make operational policies requiring that the loss of agricultural land be compensated with alternative land, especially in the face of increasing pressure on land and the limited availability of arable land as well as its high price. This is despite the fact that most non- land-for-land programmes have failed to foster successful self-employment and other non-land-based livelihood strategies, especially in the critical areas of employment, skills, and capacity building.
- Forced displacement usually results in people being transplanted from a social ecology in which they were primary actors to one in which they are aliens; they are not only very vulnerable but also end up in most cases as an underclass in their new socio-cultural background.
- Communities of displaced people are invariably fragmented and randomly atomised, tearing as under kinship and social networks and traditional support systems. Communities and often even large families are broken up and resettled over a wide area. The outcomes are psychological pathologies and alcoholism etc, common among displaced populations. It has been documented that this greatly enhanced psychological and psycho-social stress caused by involuntary resettlement heightens morbidity and immorality.
- The special vulnerabilities and specific needs of indigenous and tribal peoples have been inadequately addressed. Resettlement sites have been under-prepared in terms of basic amenities and essential infrastructure such as health, schooling, and credit.
- Generally, displacement as result of acquisition is legally sanctioned while, with few exceptions, there is no legal framework that governs the process of displacement itself.

- Both in the case of national laws and international agency policies, there has been a wide gap between the laws and policies and their actual implementation. Cases include the Sardar Sarovar Project where apparently progressive state government and World Bank policies have failed to prevent widespread impoverishment and suffering among displaced people, and the Three Gorges Project in China where a national resettlement law has not prevented numerous problems from emerging.

In many cases the focus of resettlement programmes is simply to get people out of the project sites as quickly and smoothly as possible. Once people are relocated or even shifted out of the project site, the resettlement programme usually fizzles out or loses momentum. The resettled people are most vulnerable to be forgotten once the physical relocation is complete[3]. Forced relocation disrupts, or even destroys, social organisation of production, networks of relationships, allocation of resources, and an entire complex of rights, individual and communal. These cannot be restored by the mere provision of alternative land and housing. Once it becomes known that people are to be relocated, a process of deferred investment sets in on the part of those to be resettled, as well as of outside sources, such as government and entrepreneurs. People in areas from which resettlement is to take place thus become poorer, even before they are moved. Resettlement in the absence of active development initiatives is thus likely to become impoverishment - the opposite of what it is intended to be. Resettlement of displaced people is thus a process that is acknowledged as entailing several risks. As discussed above, Cernea[4] identifies the risks as landlessness, joblessness, homelessness, marginalisation, increased morbidity and mortality, food insecurity, loss of access to common property and services, and social disarticulation. These risks render resettlement inherently problematic, and indeed impoverishment and disempowerment have been the rule than the exception with respect to resettled people around the world simply restoring the status quo in terms of material assets will thus leave people worse off than before. Therefore the main objective of a resettlement programme must be to improve the standard of living and not just restoration of pre-relocation standards of living. While the restoration of standards is still echoed in several resettlement programmes there is enough evidence to indicate that this goal is limited and inadequate[5].

Rehabilitation and Development

Rehabilitation can be envisioned as a process that would reverse the risks of resettlement. Cernea suggests a risk and reconstruction model of rehabilitation that would be marked by a series of transitions from:

- landlessness to land-based resettlement;
- joblessness to re-employment;
- food insecurity to safe nutrition;
- homelessness to house reconstruction;
- increased morbidity and mortality to improved health and well being, and
- social disarticulation and deprivation of common property resources to community reconstruction and social inclusion.[6]

Rehabilitation is only possible where development takes place. Thus, resettlement must be planned as an integral part of the comprehensive development project[7]. In this sense rehabilitation is really an outcome of resettlement that is conceived not as physical relocation or mere restoration of incomes but as development. This brings us to the question of development in the context of resettlement and rehabilitation. One useful way of understanding development in the context of resettlement and rehabilitation of negatively affected people is, in terms of the real freedoms that the citizens enjoy, to pursue the objectives they have reason to value, and in this sense the expansion of human capability can be, broadly, seen as the central feature of the process of development[8]. A resettlement programme in order to qualify as development must therefore centre around:

(i) enhancement of capabilities; and

(ii) the expansion of social opportunities

This would mean that resettlement with development entails questions of resources and rights that would affect the quality of life of the people. The success of development programmes cannot be judged merely in terms of their effects on incomes and outputs, and must, at a basic level, focus on the lives that people can lead. This would mean: (i) tangible benefits like lower morbidity and mortality, an increasing level of education, increasing incomes through opportunities for employment and livelihood; and (ii) empowering the displaced people through building capacities by their participation in the entire decision-making process of the development project and resettlement.

Mining and Displacement

In the global era, mining has become another very important source of investment and profit for the private sector. Mining-induced displacement and resettlement (MIDR) has become a major risk from the point of view of social sustainability. Scanty information on the MIDR indicates a very high displacement in the past and even increasing trend in the future due to rich mineral deposits which are found in areas with relatively high density of politically powerless populations. In India, most of the affected people are the tribal and other indigenous people[9].

The size of the mines at present is taking a gigantic leap as compared to over the years. Coal caters to a third India's energy needs. Coal mines have expanded from an average of 150 acres in the 1960s to 800 acres in the 1980s over the last three decades due to shift from underground to opencast mines for exploiting lower quality coal that resulted over some 1500 acres of land as open cast mines require more land and induce displacement of more persons without even creating jobs to absorb people. Industries and mines give a job each to the families they displace but ever since the mechanisation process starts, the scope of absorbing people subtly begins shrinking[10].

Company-wise

Company	*Total Land Acquired*	*Total Tenancy Land Acquired*	*Tenancy Land in Possession*
Eastern Coalfields Limited (ECL)	13093	12022	9145
Bharat Coking Coal Limited (BCCL)	4280	3857	1937
Central Coalfields Limited (CCL)	35736	12758	4883
South Eastern Coalfields Limited (SECL)	20538	12812	11873
Western Coalfields Limited (WCL)	19785	17089	14330
Northern Coalfields Limited (NCL)	15948	5612	5275
Mahanadi Coalfields Limited (MCL)	19965	9180	4252
North Eastern Coalfields Limited (NECL)	25041	41.47	41.47
Total	**154386**	**73371.47**	**51736.47**

Obviously, the landless people are mainly dependent on Common Property Resources (CPRs) and are outside the purview of compensation of any type. The land area required, in turn, is directly proportional to the type of projects undertaken. Some examples are cited below:

(i) In the power sector, the NTPC Ltd. and Uttar Pradesh Rajya Vidyut Nigam Ltd. (UPRVUNL), on the 22 November 2007 signed a Memorandum of Understanding (MoU) to set up a thermal power plant of 1,320 MW at Kohrarghat of Meha Tehsil in Allahabad District of east UP. The government of UP acquired a total land area of 2500 acres for setting up the plant that affected the livelihood of 469 settled households. This adversely affected agricultural output and food security.

(ii) To set up a 3500 MW gas-based power plant with an estimated project cost of Rs 25,000 cr in Dadri Region in Ghaziabad District, Hapur Tehsil, in western UP, the Government of Uttar Pradesh acquired about 1,011 hectare of land in the year 2004. Most of the land acquired was earlier used for agricultural purposes. The major assets covered in land acquisition were canals, ponds and wells. Land acquisition in Dadri was estimated to have led to displacement of over 6,000 families.

(iii) POSCO, the world's fourth largest South Korean steel company, had signed a MoU with the Government of Odisha in 2005 to set up a plant, near Paradip Port in Odisha's Jagatsinghpur District that produce 12 million tons of steel per annum. Approx. 3,000 people were displaced. The people, resisting land acquisition, opined that the project would destroy their livelihood that thrives on shrimp farming and cultivation of betel leaves, a highly profitable crop. The strugglers, against PASCO's proposed plant, rejected the rehabilitation package for the displaceable, announced by the Odisha Government[11].

Government s Effort towards Rehabilitation and Resettlement of Internally Displaced Persons (IDPs)

In India, the problem of land acquisition and payment of compensation is handled by the colonial Land Acquisition Act, 1894.

The land acquisition procedure has become a complex one, prohibiting the payment of fair compensation to project ousters. The operation of the said Act has given the state the authority to abuse power and fix the rate of compensation in a most arbitrary manner[12].

To address various issues related to land acquisition and rehabilitation and resettlement comprehensively the Department of Land Resources has formulated a National Rehabilitation and Resettlement Policy, 2007. The new policy has been notified in the Official Gazette and has become operative with effect from the 31 October 2007; based on which many State Governments have their own Rehabilitation and Resettlement Policies.

- The National Resettlement and Rehabilitation Policy (NRRP) 2007 is applicable to all development projects leading to involuntary resettlement of people.
- The policy aims to minimise displacement and promote, as far as possible, non-displacing or least displacing alternatives.
- The policy also aims to ensure adequate rehabilitation package and expeditious implementation of the rehabilitation process with the active participation of those affected.
- The policy also recognises the need for protecting the weaker sections of the society especially members of the Scheduled Castes and Scheduled Tribes[13] .

To give legal backing to the policy, the Cabinet also decided to bring legislation on the lines of Resettlement and Rehabilitation Policy and to suitably amend the Land Acquisition Act, 1894. In this direction, Government has introduced two bills on similar lines in Lok Sabha in 2009 named as the Land Acquisition (Amendment) Bill, 2007 and the Rehabilitation and Resettlement Bill, 2007. Both of the Bills lapsed with the dissolution of the 14th Lok Sabha.

The Right to Fair Compensation and Transparency in Land Acquisition, Rehabilitation and Resettlement Bill, 2012

In May 2011, the National Advisory Council recommended combining the provisions of Land Acquisition and Rehabilitation and Resettlement (R&R) within a single Bill. In this direction, the Right to Fair Compensation and Transparency in Land Acquisition, Rehabilitation and Resettlement Bill, 2012 (formerly known as the

Land Acquisition, Rehabilitation and Resettlement Bill, 2011) was introduced in Lok Sabha on 7 September 2011. The Bill was passed on 29 August 2013 in Lok Sabha and on 5 September 2013 in Rajya Sabha. In the next few months, the Centre will be framing rules under the Act and it would be notified early next year[14] .

The landmark Bill on the Right to Fair Compensation and Transparency in Land Acquisition, Rehabilitation and Resettlement 2013 brings an end to the era of forced land acquisition. Integrating land acquisition with rehabilitation and resettlement and bringing transparency in the process of acquisition, compensation, and rehabilitation as a matter of right is a historic step. It was important to have a law to prevent forcible land acquisitions which have increased during the last few decades due to big industrial and development projects. Providing fair compensation and R&R to the farmers, land-owners and livelihood losers in all acquisitions becomes critical in the context of increasing alienation, displacement, deprivation, and disentitlement to the resources of livelihood. Some salient features of the Bill are as under:

Salient Features of the Bill

- Consent of 80 per cent of landowners required in case of land acquired by private companies and 70 per cent for land acquired under Public Private Partnership (PPP) model for public purpose.
- Mandatory Social Impact Analysis (SIA) to assess nature of public interest and estimation of socio-economic impact prior to acquisition.
- Land cannot be vacated until the entire compensation is awarded to the affected parties.
- Companies can lease the land instead of purchasing it.
- Private companies to provide for rehabilitation and resettlement if land acquired through private negotiations is more than 50 acres in urban areas and 100 acres in rural areas.
- Affected families include farm labour, tenants, sharecroppers and workers on the piece of land for three years prior to the acquisition.

- Compensation should be house, one time allowance and (either Rs 5 lakh or a job or inflation adjusted Rs 2,000 per month for 20 years) for the affected family.
- Compensation of four times the market value in rural areas and twice in urban areas will be given to affected families.

Michael Cernea, a sociologist based at the World Bank who has researched development induced displacement and resettlement for two decades, points out that being forcibly ousted from one's land and habitat carries with it the risk of becoming poorer than before displacement. Those displaced 'are supposed to receive compensation of their lost assets, and effective assistance to re-establish themselves productively; yet this does not happen for a large portion of oustees.' Cernea's impoverishment risk and reconstruction model proposes that 'the onset of impoverishment can be represented through a model of eight interlinked potential: risks intrinsic to displacement'. These are:

1. **Landlessness**: Expropriation of land removes the main foundation upon which people's productive systems, commercial activities and livelihoods are constructed. This is the principle form of de-capitalisation and pauperisation of displaced people, as they lose both natural and or a human-made capital.
2. **Joblessness**: The risk of losing wage employment is very high both in urban and rural displacements for those employed in enterprises, services or agriculture. Yet, creating new jobs is difficult and requires substantial investment. Unemployment or underemployment among resettlers often endures long after physical relocation has been completed.
3. **Homelessness**: Loss of shelter tends to be only temporary for many resettlers; but, for some, homelessness worsening in their housing standards remains a lingering condition. In a broader cultural sense, loss of a family's individual home and the loss of a group's cultural space tend to result in alienation and status deprivation.
4. **Marginalisation**: Marginalisation occurs when families lose economic power and spiral on a 'downward mobility' path. Many individuals cannot use their earlier acquired skills at the new location; human capital is lost or rendered inactive

or obsolete. Economic marginalisation is often accompanied by social and psychological marginalisation, expressed in a drop in social status, in resettlers' loss of confidence in society and in themselves, a feeling of injustice, and deepened vulnerability.

5. **Food Insecurity**: Forced uprooting increases the risk that people will fall into temporary or chronic undernourishment, defined as calorie-protein intake levels below the minimum necessary for normal growth and work.
6. **Increased Morbidity and Mortality**: Massive population displacement threatens to cause serious decline in health levels. Displacement-induced social stress and psychological trauma are sometimes accompanied by the outbreak of relocation related illnesses, particularly parasitic and vector-borne diseases such as malaria. Unsafe water supply and improvised sewage systems increase vulnerability to epidemics and chronic diarrhea, dysentery, and so on. The weakest segments of the demographic spectrum infants, children, and the elderly are affected most strongly.
7. **Loss of Access to Common Property**: For poor people, loss of access to the common property assets that belonged to relocated communities (pastures, forest lands, water bodies, burial grounds, quarries, and so on) result in significant deterioration in income and livelihood levels.
8. **Social Disintegration**: The fundamental feature of forced displacement is that it causes a profound unraveling of existing patterns of social organisation. This unraveling occurs at many levels. When people are forcibly moved, production systems are dismantled. Long-established residential communities and settlements are disorganised, while kinship groups and family systems are often scattered. Life-sustaining informal social networks that provide mutual help are rendered non-functional. Trade linkages between producers and their customer base are interrupted and local labor markets are disrupted. Formal and informal associations and self-organised services are wiped out by the sudden scattering of their membership. Traditional management systems tend to lose their leaders.The coerced abandonment

of symbolic markers (such as ancestral shrines and graves) or of spatial contexts (such as mountains and rivers considered holy, or sacred trails) cuts off some of the physical and psychological linkages with the past and saps at the roots of the peoples' cultural identity. The cumulative effect is that the social fabric is torn apart.

9. **Loss of Access to Community Services**: This could include anything from health clinics to educational facilities but especially costly both in the short-term and long-term are lost or delayed opportunities for the education of children.
10. **Violation of Human Rights**: Displacement from one's habitual residence and the loss of property without fair

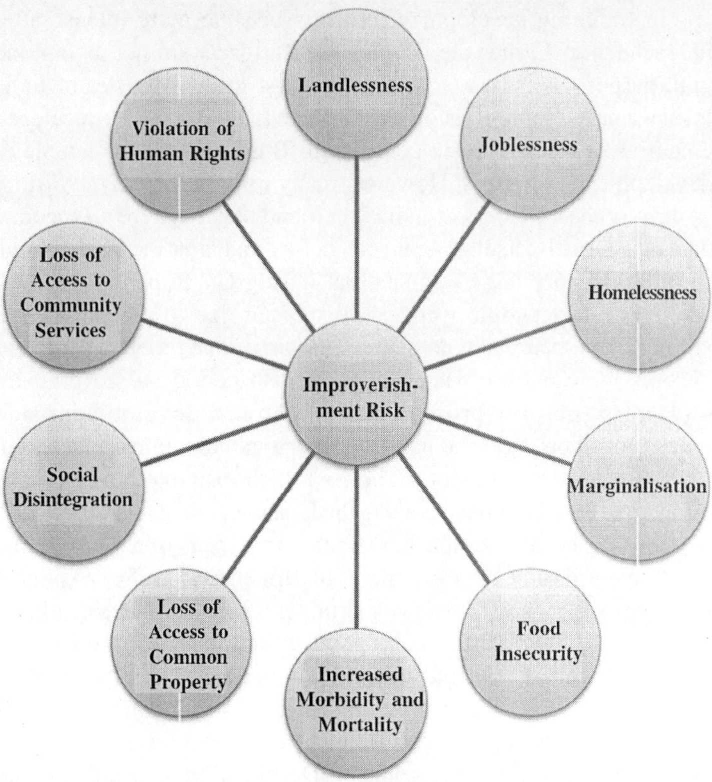

Figure 5.1 – Impact of Displacement: Michael Cernea

compensation can, in itself, constitute a violation of human rights. In addition to violating economic and social rights, listed above, arbitrary displacement can also lead to violations of civil and political rights, including: arbitrary arrest, degrading treatment or punishment, temporary or permanent disenfranchisement and the loss of one's political voice. Finally, displacement carries not only the risk of human rights violations at the hands of state authorities and security forces but also the risk of communal violence when new settlers move in amongst existing populations. The impact of Displacement, to put it in other terms, by Michael Cernea has been placed in figure 5.1.

Development Process In India

In India the development projects became more intense after independence. Earlier the development projects are not as big and multipurpose as it is now a day. The first Prime Minister of India Pt. Jawaharlal Nehru's vision was to make India at par with developed countries of the world. He considered 'Big Dams' as the temple of developmental progress. However, many examples from the history of development process in India it is found that there are no accurate data of internally displaced persons before and after the British came to India. History has examples that during Gupta period (of third century) many people were got displaced due to developmental projects. But there were no data of that time. The problem started to become more intense when during British period the government undertook certain projects for economic development and industrialisation e.g. establishment of tea garden, coffee plantation, township, oil refineries etc. The first such example however was building of Jai Chammand pond in the Udaipur area of the Rajasthan[15]. It needs to be mentioned here that apart from other things the government during the time frame of British period they exploited forest resources, river systems and mineral base and have displaced many people. But at that time as population was very sparse in India so people need not have to think much and just live in some other place. It took a serious turn only when the British government in order to have an easy land acquisition system formulated Permanent Settlement Act, 1793. According to Dadabhai Naoroji although no data regarding the IDPs were found at that time however there were more than 350 lakh people displaced at that time in the name of development projects. Eventually because of that in many areas rebel started fight against the British Government. The Mulchi Peta Movement in Maharashtra during 1920s was one such example[16]. After independence of India due to emotional sentiment and patriotic feelings among the people whatever development project government started it was accepted without any doubt and criticism. Sometimes even if someone becomes serious about the negative outcome of the project he or she had compelled to silent under patriotic feeling and nationalistic emotions. During 1950s and 60s in order to made India parallel to the western countries the government ignored negative impact of the development related project. The masses believed that the development projects will bring back prosperity and happiness. Many of them happily gave up their land in the belief of overall development of the country and of their own. The national consensus and patriotic feeling was so strong nobody dares to go against the decision of the government[17]. But, as time passes this has started to become a serious issue. Studies carried out in development projects sites started to highlight the growing number of displaced people and their deteriorating economic situation, social implications etc.

The industrialisation process is said to be the index for development of any country. However, development induced displacement is one of the most troublesome yet global phenomena which are experienced by millions of people. Each year millions of people rendered homeless due to development projects in their country. In the name of building dams, roads, reservoirs, mining, railways, industries millions of people became homeless and displaced. These people lost their homes for the benefits of the other. As this people never cross the border of their territory they are regarded as Internally Displaced Persons (IDPs). It is quite understood that a country can be developed only if its economic sector is developed but by affecting a vulnerable sector in the name of development is not development at all. Earlier it was easy to plan any development projects as population was very few and there were in abundance of land moreover there was no such mega projects to deal with at that time. But as time passes with growing demands from population the government has no other option but to choose for mega projects like multi-purpose dams, bigger industrial zones, more and more widening of roads, railways etc.

Types of Development Process

The development projects ultimately lead to two types of displacement- direct and indirect displacement. In direct displacement process there are some people who will be directly affected by the project. The directly displaced people any how got the compensation in both cash and kind (although not satisfactory) and have legal rights to demand protection from the authority. In case of indirect displacement the persons will not be evacuated directly. But these people usually dwells on these areas and dependent on the forest and in nearby areas. They may be people who has shops, the vendors, the daily wage earner, depend on forest for logs, herbs, vegetables and fruits, medicinal plants etc. When project installed these people eventually lost its traditional business, its market and related economy. Their means of livelihood got changed. Many started searching jobs in cities. This again leads to the pressure in cities. Many a times these people started to live within the vicinity of the project area as slum dwellers. It made an insecure life for them. During the time of Bhopal Gas Tragedy most of people who died there live in a slum area near the industry[18]. The people who are affected indirectly by a development project can be termed as Project Affected Persons (PAPs). The point here is that as we do not know how many people are indirectly affected by a project so many a times wrong judgments happened. Moreover, sometime installation of a small rig near paddy field by Oil companies leads to disaster for the family and those who dwells in those fields suffers. The accidental spill of oil leads disaster for farmers in the long run. Both direct and indirect displacement is cause of concern for the government. Both should need to provide with not only economic assistance but also how they could be accumulated in the long run in the process of development is the responsibility of the planners.

The Paradigm Shift

This all shows the changes of policy of the government towards development programmes. The Government is now set up Environment Tribunals to see the environmental impact of any project.

The setting up of various committees before considering any project is very new idea of government to tackle the issue of IDPs. This is nothing but shifting of policies.

Notes

1. Bartolome, Leopoldo & Danklmaier Christine The Experience with Dams and Resettlement in Argentina.
2. Cernea, Michael M: Impoverishment or Social Justice? A Model for Planning Resettlement in Mathur, H.M. and Marsden, David (ed.) Development Projects and Impoverishment Risks, 1998.
3. Argentina Report (WCD), 1999. Danklemaier: Displacement, Resettlement, Rehabilitation, Reparation and Development, WCD Report, Argentina. Bartolome, J.L. & Mohha, C.
4. Cernea, Michael M: Impoverishment or Social Justice? A Model for Planning Resettlement in Mathur, H.M. and Marsden, David (ed.) Development Projects and Impoverishment Risks, 1998.
5. Scudder, Thayer: Social Impacts of Large Dams in Large Dams; Learning from the Past, Looking at the Future, IUCN/WB, Gland, 1997.
6. Cernea, Michael M: Impoverishment or Social Justice? A Model for Planning Resettlement in Mathur, H.M. and Marsden, David (ed.) Development Projects and Impoverishment Risks, 1998.
7. Jain, L.C. 1999, 2000. Comments on draft Thematic Review 1.3, Sao Paulo Minutes of the Commission Meeting, September 1999.
8. Dreze, J & Sen, A. 1996. India: Economic Development and Social Opportunity, New Delhi, Oxford University Press.
9. Deogharia, Parkash Chandra: Development, Displacement and Deprivation, New Delhi 2012, p. 7.
10. *Ibid*, pp. 7-8.
11. Mishra, Nihar Ranjan: *Displacement and Rehabilitation – Solutions for the Future*, Bhopal, 2012, pp. 280-283.
12. *Op.cit*, Deogharia, Parkash Chandra, p. 13.
13. *Op.cit*, Deogharia, Parkash Chandra, p. 13.
14. www.sustainuance.com dated 17.9.2013.
15. Ganguly, Thukral Enakshi and Singh,M.(1995): *Dams And Displaced In India,* in Hari Mohan Mathur And Michael Cernea (Ed.)*Development Displacement And Resettlement: Focus On Asian Experiences* (New Delhi: Vikas Publishing House Pvt. Ltd), p. 94.
16. Bharali and Fernandes (2007), *Unnayan Bonam Sthanantor, a Qualitative and Quantitative Study of Land Acquisition and Development in Assam From 1947-2000*, (Guwahati:NESSRC Publication), p. 13.

17. Negi, N.S. and Ganguly, S. (2011): "Developmental projects vs internally displaced populations in India : A literature based appraisal" Paper presented at the ESF-UniBi-ZiF Research conference on "environmental change and Migration: from vulnerabilities to capabilities, Bad Salzuflen, Germany, 5-9 December, 2010.

    COMCAD Arbiets Papiere- working paper no. 103, 2011.

    (http://www.unibielefeld.de/tdrc/ag_comcad/downloads/workingpaper_103_negi_ganguly.pdf) retrieved on 23 September, 2013, pp. 5-7.
18. Biswal, T. (2006), *Human Rights Gender and Environment*, (New Delhi:Viva publishing House), p. 465.

Chapter 6

An Opinion Study

The opinion study deals with data interpretation as provided by the respondents. For data collection, 500 respondents are the interviewed. For this purpose, scientific methods comprising of survey and questionnaire techniques are used. Here to make it foursquare random sampling method was used. The whole nucleus was taken from industrial displaced persons of different parts of Odisha. Statistical techniques like X^{2-} test, rank analysis, correlation etc, have been used to justify the strength of the obtained results. The results was obtained by using IBM SPSS 20.0 package that is widely used and acclaimed software. The questionnaire consists of 27 questions. Out of 500 respondents, 20 respondents have no knowledge about Rehabilitation Policy of Government. Hence, their responses are ignored while analysing the data. Effectively the nucleus (n) of the data is 480.

For better analysis, Question has been put before the respondents to know the basic idea about the concept. In the question, the respondents are requested to tell the knowledge about the Rehabilitation Policy of the Government.

Table 6.1: Knowledge about Rehabilitation Policy of Government

		Frequency	*Per cent*	*Valid Per cent*	*Cumulative Per cent*
Valid	Yes	480	96	96	96
	No	20	4	4	100.0
	Total	**500**	**100.0**	**100.0**	

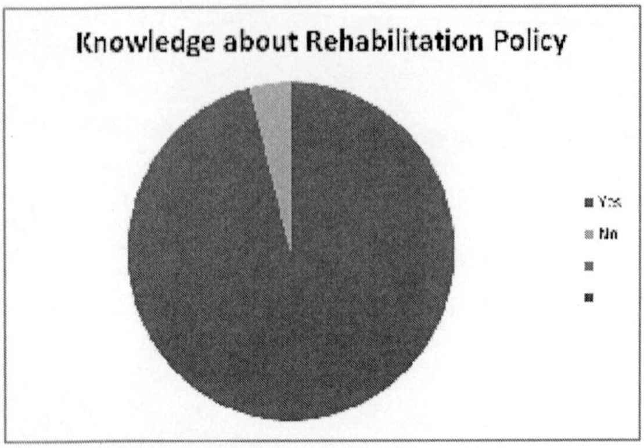

Figure 6.1: Knowledge about Rehabilitation Policy of Government.

The Table 6.1 showed that the responses have been obtained for getting a firsthand knowledge of respondents regarding the Rehabilitation Policy of India. Data analysis showed majority (96 per cent) have knowledge on Rehabilitation Policy. Similarly, 4 per cent have no knowledge. Hence, majority have knowledge on Rehabilitation Policy. In above Table No 6.1 the scores are given.

Table 6.2: Necessity Of Displacement for Setting up Industry.

		Frequency	*Per cent*	*Valid Per cent*	*Cumulative Per cent*
Valid	Yes	183	38.1	38.1	38.1
	No	297	61.9	61.9	100.0
	Total	**480**	**100.0**	**100.0**	

With regard to the query about their knowledge, a question was asked to the respondents about their thinking pattern for setting up industries at the cost of displacement. Out of the total 480 respondents, 61.9 per cent are against displacement for industrialisation. 38.1 per cent respondents agree to displacement for industrialisation. From Table 6.2 the study indicates that majority of respondents are against displacement for setting up industry.

Table 6.3: Justification of Resentment for Setting up Industry.

		Frequency	*Per cent*	*Valid Per cent*	*Cumulative Per cent*
Valid	Yes	474	98.8	98.8	98.8
	No	6	1.2	1.2	100.0
	Total	**480**	**100.0**	**100.0**	

To be more specific another question has been asked about to study the justification of resentment for industrialisation. From the study it reveals that maximum 98.8 per cent respondents are of the opinion that resentment movement is justified against the industries. Whereas only 1.3 per cent respondents are of the view that resentment movement is not justified.

Table 6.4: Participation in Resentment Movement.

		Frequency	*Per cent*	*Valid Per cent*	*Cumulative Per cent*
Valid	Yes	360	75.0	75.0	75.0
	No	120	25.0	25.0	100.0
	Total	**480**	**100.0**	**100.0**	

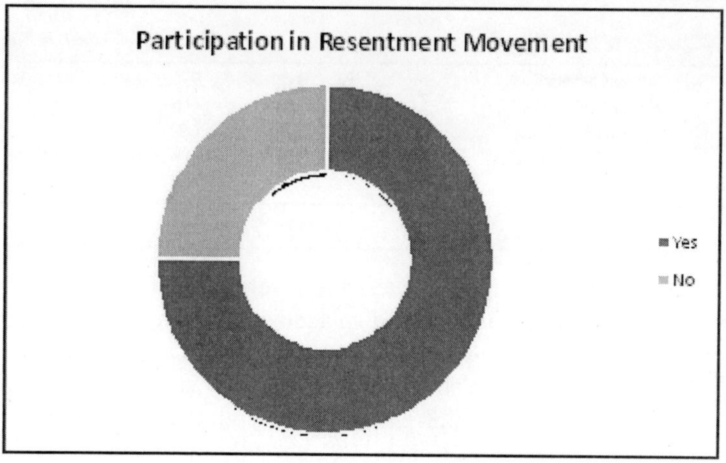

Figure 6.2: Participation in Resentment Movement

Further, a question was asked to test the level of direct participation of respondents in the resentment movement. Out of the 480 respondents 360 (75 per cent) have directly participated in the resentment movement as an affected person. 120 (25 per cent) respondents have not participated in the resentment movement. So maximum number of affected people are involved in direct resentment movement against industrialisation.

Table 6.5: Village Agitation

		Frequency	*Per cent*	*Valid Per cent*	*Cumulative Per cent*
Valid	Yes	414	86.25	86.25	86.25
	No	66	13.75	13.75	100.0
	Total	**480**	**100.0**	**100.0**	

From the above table it is found that, in 86.3 per cent cases there was an agitation by the villagers (of the respondents) against industries.

Table 6.6: Level of Satisfaction due to Displacement.

Q6

		Frequency	*Per cent*	*Valid Per cent*	*Cumulative Per cent*
Valid	Strongly Satisfied	88	18.3	18.3	18.3
	Adequately Satisfied	142	29.6	29.6	47.9
	Undecided	32	6.7	6.7	54.6
	Some how dissatisfied	95	19.8	19.8	74.4
	Strongly dissatisfied	123	25.6	25.6	100.0
	Total	**480**	**100.0**	**100.0**	

A question was asked to test the level of satisfaction of the respondents due to industrial displacement. A five point rating scale will measure the satisfaction level. Out 480 respondents 18.3 per cent people are strongly satisfied, 29.6 per cent people are adequately satisfied, 19.8 per cent respondents are somehow dissatisfied, 25.6 per cent people are strongly dissatisfied. While 6.7 per cent are undecided.

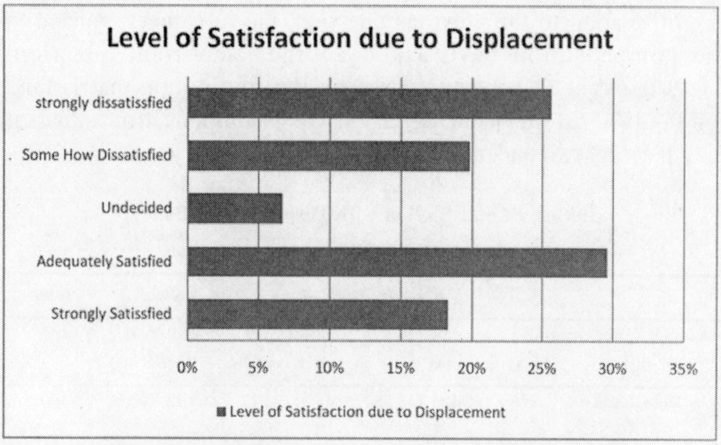

Figure 6.3: Level of Satisfaction due to Displacement

Table 6.7: Rehabilitation Measures

Rehabilitation Measures	*Frequency*	*Per cent*
Land for land	311	64.79
Cash Compensation	217	45.21
Jobs in industry	11	2.29

The fact has been put in the figure 6.4

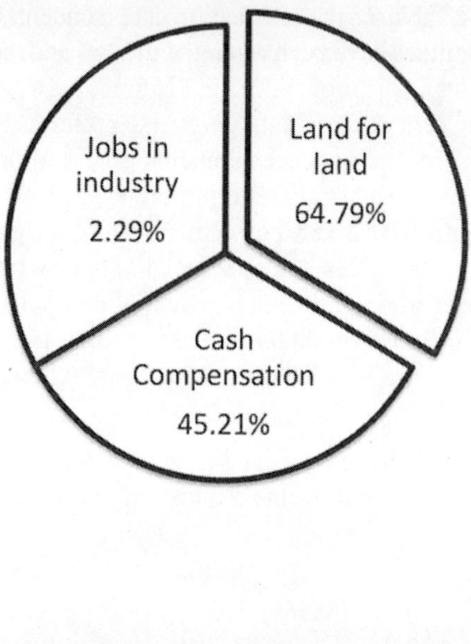

In relation to the previous question, the researchers related to the compensation have asked another important question. 64.79 per cent respondents agree on the first option that is land for land. 45.21 per cent agree on cash compensation and rest 2.29 per cent respondents are getting job in industry.

Table 6.8: Satisfaction with Displacement Policy

Q8

	Rank 1	*Rank 2*	*Rank 3*	*Total*
Financial Compensation	117 (24.37 per cent)	134 (27.92 per cent)	229 (47.71 per cent)	480
Substitute Land	105 (21.88 per cent)	183 (38.12 per cent)	192 (40.00 per cent)	480
Service in Industry	258 (53.75 per cent)	163 (33.95 per cent)	59 (12.30 per cent)	480

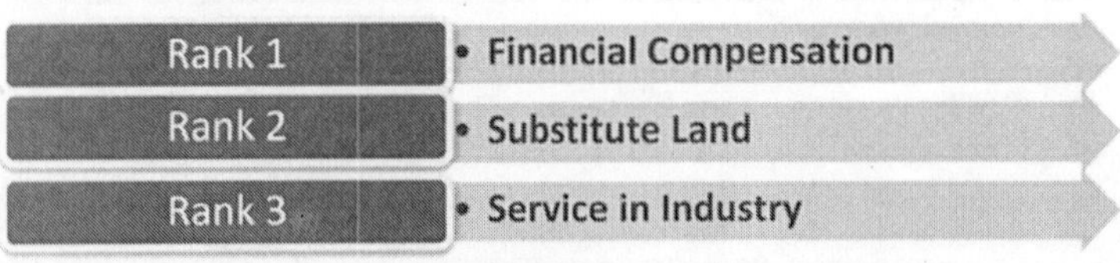

Figure 6.5: Rank Levels of Satisfaction with Displacement Policy

In the above Table 6.8 the satisfaction of respondents with different displacement policies have been arranged in rows and the preferential opinions towards them in columns. In the above table 24.37 per cent respondents gives 1st preference to financial compensation, 27.92 per cent respondents give 2nd preference and 47.71 per cent respondents give 3rd preference as well. Again the in case of substitute land 21.88 per cent respondents gives 1st rank, 38.12 per cent people gives 2nd rank and 40 per cent people chooses as 3rd rank. 53.75 per cent respondents out of 480 put 1st rank to the option service in industry, 33.95 per cent people gives it 2nd rank and 12.305 people gives as 3rd rank. Also figure 6.5 may referred for better clarity.

Displacements have a great impact on the life style of the displaced persons. To add to this a question was asked to know the post-displacement impact on their life style. For collecting firsthand information the respondents are asked to rank the areas of changes in life style.. Six areas have been given those are: (a) Financial Status, (b) Livelihood, (c) Education of Children, (d) Health care benefits, (e) Food Security, (f) Improved Communication. The ranking information are shown in the following analysis table elaborately:

Table 6.9: Impact of Displacement on Life Style

Q10

	Rank 1	*Rank 2*	*Rank 3*	*Rank 4*	*Rank 5*	*Rank 6*	*Total*
Financial Status	236 (49.17 per cent)	143 (29.79 per cent)	55 (11.46 per cent)	25 (5.20 per cent)	13 (2.71 per cent)	8 (1.67 per cent)	480
Livelihood	123 (25.62 per cent)	164 (34.16 per cent)	87 (18.13 per cent)	53 (11.04 per cent)	31 (6.46 per cent)	22 (4.59 per cent)	480
Education of Children	41 (8.54 per cent)	62 (12.92 per cent)	128 (26.67 per cent)	96 (20.00 per cent)	82 (17.08 per cent)	71 (14.79 per cent)	480
Health Care Benefits	21 (4.37 per cent)	43 (8.96 per cent)	72 (15.00 per cent)	87 (18.12 per cent)	165 (34.38 per cent)	92 (19.17 per cent)	480
Food Security	47 (9.79 per cent)	51 (10.63 per cent)	91 (18.96 per cent)	154 (32.08 per cent)	58 (12.08 per cent)	79 (16.46 per cent)	480
Improved Communication	12 (2.50 per cent)	17 (3.55 per cent)	47 (9.79 per cent)	65 (13.54 per cent)	131 (27.29 per cent)	208 (43.33 per cent)	480

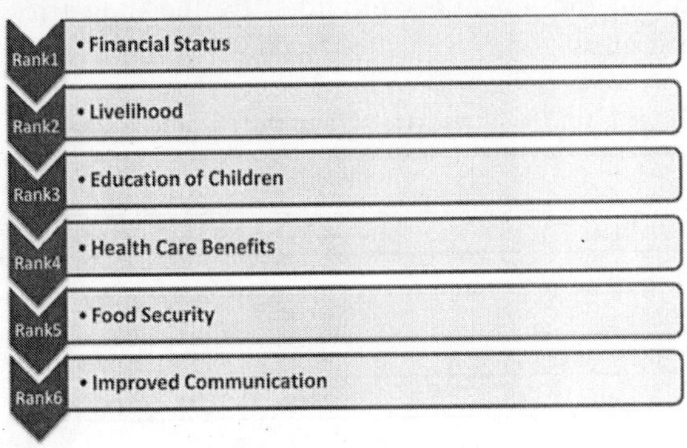

Figure 6.6 : Ranking of Impact of Displacement on Life Style

In the above table the changes of life style in different areas after displacements are ranked according to the response. Out 480 respondents 49.17 per cent gives 1st rank, 29.79 per cent gives 2nd rank, 11.46 per cent gives 3rd rank, 5.20 per cent give 4th rank 2.71 per cent gives 5th rank and 1.67 per cent respondents gives 6th rank to financial status. In case of livelihood 25.62 per cent, 34.16 per cent, 18.13 per cent, 11.04 per cent, 6.46 per cent, 4.59 per cent gives 1st, 2nd, 3rd, 4th, 5th and 6th rank respectively. In case of Education of Children 8.54 per cent people gives 1st rank, 12.92 per cent gives 2nd rank, 26.67 per cent gives 3rd rank, 20 per cent people gives 4th rank 17.08 per cent people gives 5th rank and 14.79 per cent people gives 6th rank accordingly.

Again, the respondents asked to rank the health care benefits after displacement. 4.37 per cent puts 1st rank, 8.96 per cent people put 2nd rank, 15 per cent put 3rd rank, 18.12 per cent put 4th rank, 34.38 per cent people give 5th rank and 19.17 per cent people put 6th rank to health care benefits. In case of food security 9.79 per cent respondents give 1st rank, 10.63 per cent gives it 2nd rank, 18.96 per cent gives 3rd rank, 32.08 per cent put it rank 4th, 12.08 per cent put it as rank 5th and rest 16,46 per cent people put it as 6th rank. Another area is communication facility. The respondents asked to rank the improved communication facility. Here 2.5 per cent put rank 1st, 3.55 per cent put 2nd rank, 9.79 per cent put 3rd rank, 13.54 per cent give 4th rank, 27.29 per cent give 5th rank and 43.33 per cent give 6th rank.

To be more specific about the life style changes, the scholar asked to them about the amenities provided by the industries at the rehabilitated areas.

Table 6.10: Facilities Available to the Displaced People

Items	*Frequency*	*Percentage*
Allotted Land	478	99.6
Constructed House	344	71.7
School	480	100
Hospital	465	96.9
Park	260	54.2

(Contd...)

Electricity	476	99.2
Safe Drinking Water	480	100
Bank	478	99.6
Market	472	98.3
Pucca Road	356	74.2
Post Office	476	99.2
Community Centre	356	74.2

In the Table 6.10 the scholar asked the available amenities in the rehabilitated areas. As corollary to the above question another question asked about different facilities. In the Table 6.8 the data shows about the allotted land given to the affected people. 99.6 per cent people are provided with land. The above table shows the data about constructed house. Out of 480 people 71.7 per cent people are provided with constructed house.

School facilities are available to everybody. The next table shows the medical facilities given to the affected areas. 96 per cent people are getting medical facilities. 26 per cent people are getting park Facility. Rest of the 74 per cent people are not getting recreation facilities. Electricity, drinking water and banking facility is available to 100 per cent people of the affected area. Market facility is available to 96 per cent of people. Pucca Road is given to 38 per cent of the total population. Post office facility is available to 98 per cent of the respondents, while community centre is available to only 38 per cent of the people.

Table 6.11: Identity Proof

Identity Proof	*Frequency*	*Per cent*
Voter ID	478	99.6
Ration Card	409	85.2
Adhar Card	342	71.25
BPL Card	86	17.9
ATM-cum-Debit Card	310	64.6
Credit Card	12	2.5

In response to the question 99.6 per cent people are having Voter ID. Table 6.11 shows 85.2 per cent people have ration card. 71.3 per cent respondents have Aadhar Card. 17.9 per cent people are having BPL card. 64.6 per cent people have ATM card and 2.5 per cent people out of 480 respondents have Credit cards.

Comparison of Status of Displaced Persons before and after Displacement

Table 6.12: Financial Status

		Frequency	*Per cent*	*Valid Per cent*	*Cumulative Per cent*
Valid	Imp	258	53.8	53.8	53.8
	Unc	16	3.3	3.3	57.1
	Det	206	42.9	42.9	100.0
	Total	**480**	**100.0**	**100.0**	

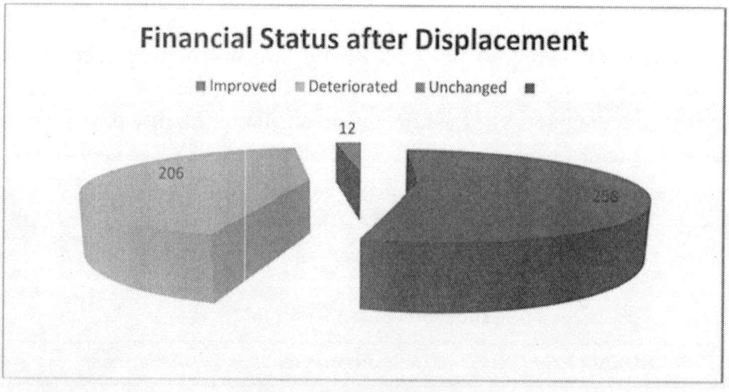

Figure 6.7: Financial Status

Table 6.12 shows that the financial status of 53.8 per cent respondents improved, while 42.9 per cent think that their financial status deteriorated due to displacement. 3.3 per cent respondents also feel that displacement has no impact on their financial status.

Table 6.13: Livelihood

		Frequency	*Per cent*	*Valid Per cent*	*Cumulative Per cent*
Valid	Imp	262	54.6	54.6	54.6
	Unc	28	5.8	5.8	60.4
	Det	190	39.6	39.6	100.0
	Total	**480**	**100.0**	**100.0**	

From Table 6.13 it is found that there is an improvement in livelihood in 54.6 per cent cases and deterioration in 39.6 per cent cases. 5.8 per cent says there is no change in livelihood.

Table 6.14: Habitat

		Frequency	*Per cent*	*Valid Per cent*	*Cumulative Per cent*
Valid	Imp	316	65.8	65.8	65.8
	Unc	20	4.2	4.2	70.0
	Det	144	30.0	30.0	100.0
	Total	**480**	**100.0**	**100.0**	

Table 6.14 shows 65.8 per cent respondent have an improvement and 30 per cent have deterioration in habitat. There is no change for 4.2 per cent respondents.

Table 6.15: Quality of House

		Frequency	*Per cent*	*Valid Per cent*	*Cumulative Per cent*
Valid	Imp	354	73.8	73.8	73.8
	Unc	40	8.3	8.3	82.1
	Det	86	17.9	17.9	100.0
	Total	**480**	**100.0**	**100.0**	

Table 6. 15 give an idea about the change in quality of house of respondents. 73.8 per cent of respondents feel there is an improvement and 17.9 per cent feel there is deterioration. 8.3 per cent feel there is no changed.

Table 6.16: Health care facilities

		Frequency	*Per cent*	*Valid Per cent*	*Cumulative Per cent*
Valid	Imp	475	99.0	99.0	99.0
	Det	5	1.0	1.0	100.0
	Total	**480**	**100.0**	**100.0**	

From the above table it is found that 99 per cent respondent have improved access to health care facilities after the displacement.

Table 6.17: Nutritional Status

		Frequency	*Per cent*	*Valid Per cent*	*Cumulative Per cent*
Valid	Imp	243	50.6	50.6	50.6
	Unc	30	6.3	6.3	56.9
	Det	207	43.1	43.1	100.0
	Total	**480**	**100.0**	**100.0**	

Table 6.17 shows 50.6 per cent respondents have an improvement in nutritional status and 43.1 per cent have deterioration in nutritional status. 6.3 per cent think their nutritional status was unchanged after displacement.

Table 6.18: No of days of Employment

		Frequency	*Per cent*	*Valid Per cent*	*Cumulative Per cent*
Valid	Imp	256	53.3	53.3	53.3
	Unc	123	25.7	25.7	79.0
	Det	101	21.0	21.0	100.0
	Total	**480**	**100.0**	**100.0**	

Table 6.18 shows that 53.3 per cent respondents think there is an improvement in number of days of employment while 21 per cent respondents think there is deterioration in number of days of employment. 25.6 per cent think there is no change.

Table 6.19 Occupation

		Frequency	*Per cent*	*Valid Per cent*	*Cumulative Per cent*
Valid	Imp	290	60.4	60.4	60.4
	Unc	57	11.9	11.9	72.3
	Det	133	27.7	27.7	100.0
	Total	**480**	**100.0**	**100.0**	

Table 6.19 give us an idea about the occupation of respondents. 60.4 per cent feel there is an improvement and 27.7 per cent feel there is deterioration. 11.9 per cent feel there is no change.

Table 6.20: Safe Drinking Water

		Frequency	*Per cent*	*Valid Per cent*	*Cumulative Per cent*
Valid	Imp	474	98.75	98.75	98.75
	Det	6	1.25	1.25	100.0
	Total	**480**	**100.0**	**100.0**	

From the above table it is found that 98.7 per cent respondent have improved access to safe drinking water after the displacement.

Table 6.21: Sanitation

		Frequency	*Per cent*	*Valid Per cent*	*Cumulative Per cent*
Valid	Imp	473	98.5	98.5	98.5
	Unc	4	.8	.8	99.4
	Det	3	.6	.6	100.0
	Total	**480**	**100.0**	**100.0**	

After displacement the sanitation facility of 98.5 per cent respondents has improved while only 0.6 per cent thinks that there is deterioration in sanitation. 0.8 per cent respondent also thinks that the sanitation facilities are unchanged.

Table 6.22: Education

		Frequency	*Per cent*	*Valid Per cent*	*Cumulative Per cent*
Valid	Imp	480	100.0	100.0	100.0

All respondents (100 per cent) feel that there is a improvement in education facilities for their children after displacement.

Table 6.23: Transport

		Frequency	*Per cent*	*Valid Per cent*	*Cumulative Per cent*
Valid	Imp	480	100.0	100.0	100.0

Table 6.23 gives us an idea that there is 100 per cent improvement in case of transportation for respondents.

Table 6.24: Communication

		Frequency	*Per cent*	*Valid Per cent*	*Cumulative Per cent*
Valid	Imp	460	95.9	95.9	95.9
	Unc	16	3.3	3.3	99.2
	Det	4	.8	.8	100.0
	Total	**480**	**100.0**	**100.0**	

From the above table it is found that 95.8 per cent respondents think that there is an improvement, 0.8 per cent thinks there is deterioration & 3.3 per cent think there is no change in communication.

Table 6.25: Life Style

		Frequency	*Per cent*	*Valid Per cent*	*Cumulative Per cent*
Valid	Imp	250	52.1	52.1	52.1
	Unc	26	5.4	5.4	57.5
	Det	204	42.5	42.5	100.0
	Total	**480**	**100.0**	**100.0**	

From Table 6. 25 it is found that there is 52.1 per cent improvement in case of overall lifestyle of respondents. 42.5 per cent respondents think that there is deterioration and only 5.4 per cent think there is no change in case of their life style.

Table 6.26 Environment

		Frequency	*Per cent*	*Valid Per cent*	*Cumulative Per cent*
Valid	Imp	195	40.6	40.6	40.6
	Unc	35	7.3	7.3	47.9
	Det	250	52.1	52.1	100.0
	Total	**480**	**100.0**	**100.0**	

Table 6.26 shows that most people (52.1 per cent) feel there is deterioration in the environment of the respondents. 40 per cent think the environment is improved while 7.3 per cent think it is unchanged.

Table 6.27: Irrigation facility

		Frequency	*Per cent*	*Valid Per cent*	*Cumulative Per cent*
Valid	Imp	106	22.1	22.1	22.1
	Unc	215	44.8	44.8	66.9
	Det	159	33.1	33.1	100.0
	Total	**480**	**100.0**	**100.0**	

From the above table it is found that only 22.1 per cent respondents think that there is an improvement, 33.1 per cent thinks there is deterioration and 44.8 per cent think there is no change in irrigation facility.

Table 6.28: Small Business/ Street Vending

		Frequency	*Per cent*	*Valid Per cent*	*Cumulative Per cent*
Valid	Imp	119	24.8	24.8	24.8
	Unc	191	39.8	39.8	64.6
	Det	170	35.4	35.4	100.0
	Total	**480**	**100.0**	**100.0**	

The data from the above Table shows that 24.8 per cent respondents think that the number of small business is improving. 39.8 per cent people say there is no change in the street vending and 35.4 per cent of people think that the condition of street vending is deteriorated due to industrial displacement.

Table 6.29: Year of Displacement

		Frequency	*Per cent*	*Valid Per cent*	*Cumulative Per cent*
Valid	1950-1970	2	0.4	0.4	0.4
	1971-1990	20	4.2	4.2	4.6
	1991-2010	421	87.7	87.7	92.3
	2011 onwards	37	7.7	7.7	100.0
	Total	**480**	**100.0**	**100.0**	

The above Table shows the maximum number of industrial displacement (87.7 per cent) occurred during the year 1991-2010. During the period of 1950-1970 2 per cent people are industrially displaced. Again during 2011 onwards 375 people are displaced.

Socio-Economic Profile: Data Analysis

Age

Age is an important factor to determine the awareness level of R&R policy among the respondents. The age profile has been classified in to five broad age groups like below 30 years, 31 to 40 years, 41 to 50 years, 51 to 60 years and above 60. The categorisation of age groups of the respondents as materialised from the study has been presented in the following Table 6.30.

Table 6.30: Age Group of the Respondents

		Frequency	*Per cent*	*Valid Per cent*	*Cumulative Per cent*
Valid	Below 30	62	12.9	12.9	12.9
	31-40	202	42.1	42.1	55.0
	41-50	180	37.5	37.5	92.5
	51-60	31	6.5	6.5	99.0
	Above 61	5	1.0	1.0	100.0
	Total	**480**	**100.0**	**100.0**	

Below 30 years age group 62 respondents resides, within 31-40 years range 202 respondents, 41-50 years 180 respondents, 51-60 years 31 respondents and the remaining 05 respondents belong to above 60 years age group.

Gender

Gender is an important factor, which also influences the knowledge level. The following table presents the sample data regarding the gender from the field study.

Table 6.31: Gender of the Respondents

		Frequency	*Per cent*	*Valid Per cent*	*Cumulative Per cent*
Valid	Male	268	55.8	55.8	55.8
	Female	212	44.2	44.2	100.0
	Total	**480**	**100.0**	**100.0**	

From the above Table No.6.31 it is found that 268 (55.8 per cent) of respondents are male members and 212 (44.2 per cent) respondents are female members.

Marital Status

The marital status of respondents needs to be taken into account while considering their demographic profile, and that have connection with the study of Policy awareness level. For this study respondents have been divided in three categories like married, unmarried and divorcee. The following table presents the sample data regarding marital status of all the respondents during the field survey.

Table 6.32: Marital Status of the Respondents

		Frequency	*Per cent*	*Valid Per cent*	*Cumulative Per cent*
Valid	Married	432	90.0	90.0	90.0
	Unmarried	44	9.2	9.2	99.2
	Divorcee	4	0.8	0.8	100.0
	Total	**480**	**100.0**	**100.0**	

The above table indicates that out of 480 total populations, 432 (90 per cent) members are married and 44 (9.2 per cent) members are unmarried. 4 members (0.8 per cent) are divorcee.

Caste

Caste is another important variable which plays a vital role and have a direct link with the knowledge level of respondents. The castes of the respondents have been classified in to three categories. They are general category, scheduled caste, and scheduled tribe respectively. The classification of the sample on the basis of caste is given below in the table.

Table 6.33: Caste Classification of the Respondents

		Frequency	*Per cent*	*Valid Per cent*	*Cumulative Per cent*
Valid	General	106	22.1	22.1	22.1
	SC	166	34.6	34.6	56.7
	ST	208	43.3	43.3	100.0
	Total	**480**	**100.0**	**100.0**	

The above table shows that out of the total 480 respondents, approximately 106 (22.1 per cent) of respondents belong to general category, 166 (34.6 per cent) belongs to Scheduled Caste, and 208 (43.3 per cent) belongs to Scheduled Tribe category. The above sample data shows that maximum people are from Scheduled Tribe category.

Educational Qualification

Educational qualifications are considered as a prime factor, which influences the knowledge. The data regarding educational background of respondents are shown from the table below:

Table 6.34: Educational Qualification of Respondents

		Frequency	*Per cent*	*Valid Per cent*	*Cumulative Per cent*
Valid	Upto 10th	286	59.6	59.6	59.6
	+2	140	29.2	29.2	88.8
	Grad.	46	9.5	9.5	98.3
	PG	8	1.7	1.7	100.0
	Total	**480**	**100.0**	**100.0**	

The above Table 6.34 shows that out of total 480 populations, 286 (59.6 per cent) are up to 10th level. Around 140 (29.2 per cent) respondents belong to + 2 level, 46 persons are from Graduation Level, and 8 (1.7 per cent) respondents belong to PG level.

Table 6.35: Residence after Displacement

		Frequency	*Per cent*	*Valid Per cent*	*Cumulative Per cent*
Valid	Urban	2	.4	.4	.4
	Semi-Urban	474	98.8	98.8	99.2
	Rural	4	.8	.8	100.0
	Total	**480**	**100.0**	**100.0**	

The above Table shows, after industrial displacement 98.8 per cent people are residing in semi-urban area. 0.4 per cent people are living in urban areas after displacement.

Monthly Income

Monthly income is also a vital factor that influences the awareness level to a greater extent. The sample data of monthly income of respondents are recorded from the survey is shown below in the Table 6.36.

Table 6.36: Monthly Income of Respondents

		Frequency	*Per cent*	*Valid Per cent*	*Cumulative Per cent*
Valid	Below 2000	85	17.7	17.7	17.7
	2000-5000	112	23.3	23.3	41.0
	5000-10000	47	9.8	9.8	50.8
	15000-25000	184	38.4	38.4	89.2
	Above 25000	52	10.8	10.8	100.0
	Total	**480**	**100.0**	**100.0**	

The data as illustrated in the table no 6.36 shows that out of 480 respondents, the monthly income of almost 85 (17.7 per cent) is below Rs 2,000, while around 112 (23.3 per cent) respondents monthly income is between Rs 2,000 to Rs 5,000. Again 47 (9.8 per cent) respondents belong to Rs 5,000 to Rs 10,000 monthly income category. 184 (38.3 per cent) persons falls within Rs 15,000 to Rs 25,000 monthly income group and remaining 52 (10.8 per cent) respondents monthly income is above Rs 25,000.

Working Sector

The link between working sector and Policy knowledge has a greater impact on the study. The 400 respondents are divided into public sector, private sector, independent sector and unorganised sector. The data is shown in the following Table 6.37:

Table 6.37: Working Sectors of Respondents

		Frequency	*Per cent*	*Valid Per cent*	*Cumulative Per cent*
Valid	Public	17	3.5	3.5	3.5
	Private	164	34.2	34.2	37.7
	Independent	92	19.2	19.2	56.9
	Unorganised	207	43.1	43.1	100.0
	Total	**480**	**100.0**	**100.0**	

The above table signifies that 17 (3.5 per cent) population belongs to public sector, 164 (34.2 per cent) respondents having are working in private sector. 92 persons working independently and 207 (43.1 per cent) population is working in unorganised sector.

Table 6.38: Using of Vehicles

Items	Frequency	Per cent
Cycle	398	82.9
Motor Cycle	238	49.6
Four Wheeler	2	.4
No Vehicle	82	17.1

82.9 per cent respondents are using cycle where as 2 per cent respondents are having four wheeler. The Data Table shows that 49.6 per cent respondents are using Motor Cycle and 17.1 per cent respondent don't have any vehicle.

Table 6.39: Gadgets used by Respondents

Gadgets Used	*Frequency*	*Per cent*
Radio	235	48.95
Television	382	79.58
Mobile Phone, Land Line	385	80.2
Computer, Laptop, Tablet	46	9.58
Digital Camera	22	4.58
Cooking Gas	303	63.12
Fridge	82	17.08
Washing Machine	38	7.91
Internet	42	8.75
Direct to Home Service	315	65.62

From the above Table (Table 6.39) we can get an idea about the gadgets used by Respondents. Out of the 480 respondents 235 (48.95 per cent) are using radio, 382 (79.58 per cent) using TV, 385 (80.2 per cent) using mobile and 46 (9.58 per cent) are using computer. 315 Respondents (65.62 per cent) are using DTH service, while 303 respondents (63.12 per cent) are using Cooking gas. Digital Camera is used by only 22 (4.58 per cent) respondents and internet is used only by 42 (8.75 per cent) respondents. 82 Respondents (17.08 per cent) are using Fridge, while only 38 respondents (7.91 per cent) are using Washing Machine.

Above Table 6.40 presents the correlation between all the demographic variables and satisfaction level of respondents due to displacement. The first column presents the correlation coefficients between satisfaction level and other demographic variables of particular interest. It is observed that the correlation between satisfaction level and age, gender, marital status, caste, education, income and working sector are significant ($P<0.05$) where as the correlation between satisfaction level and residence is not significant ($P>0.05$). The significant correlation indicates that satisfaction level of displacement is somehow related with the demographic variables as cited above. Further, the non-significant correlation of satisfaction level with demographic variable indicate that the satisfaction level in not related to that demographic variables against which correlation is not significant.

Table 6.40: Correlation between the satisfaction level on Industrial Displacement with the Demographic information

	Satisfaction level	*Age*	*Gender*	*Marital Status*	*Caste*	*Education Sector*	*Residence*	*Income*	*Working*
Satisfaction level	1	.128**	.111*	-.200**	.196**	-.556**	-.001	-.752**	.492**
Age	.128**	1	-.091*	-.396**	.031	-.177**	-.108*	-.020	.121**
Gender	.111*	-.091*	1	-.236**	.037	-.017	-.033	-.224**	.298**
Marital Status	-.200**	-.396**	-.236**	1	-.072	.137**	.099*	.137**	-.278**
Caste	.196**	.031	.037	-.072	1	-.263**	-.106*	-.264**	.126**
Education	-.556**	-.177**	-.017	.137**	-.263**	1	.074	.694**	-.334**
Residence	-.001	-.108*	-.033	.099*	-.106*	.074	1	.000	-.118**
Income	-.752*	-.020	-.224**	.137*	-.264**	.694**	.000	1	-.460**
Working Sector	.492**	.121**	.298**	-.278**	.126**	-.334**	-.118**	-.460**	1

Test of Hypotheses

Another important thing relating to the analysis is testing the fitness of hypothesis. For the purpose four hypotheses are taken. The hypotheses are given below:

- Though Orissa's draft resettlement and rehabilitation policy is an improvement on the national policy, it does not go far enough in ensuring adequate majors to the affected people.
- The development-induced –displacement process is leading to widening the gap between the rich and poor.
- The present pattern of development is the continuing powerlessness of the weaker sections due to displacement and without any benefits from these development projects.
- The Rehabilitation policy promises for the betterment of ousters but actually the effect is impoverishment, landlessness, joblessness, food insecurity, loss of common property and increased mortality.

These hypotheses are calculated with Pearson Chi Square test method with SPSS package. In Pearson test method the level of significance is 0.05. Each hypothesis tested differently by using SPSS 20.0 package.

Table 6.41: Hypothesis-1

			Q6					*Total*
			Strongly Satisfied	*Adequately Satisfied*	*Undecided*	*Some how dissatisfied*	*Strongly Satisfied*	
Q18	Yes	Count	74	84	8	0	10	176
		Per cent of Total	15.4 per cent	17.5 per cent	1.7 per cent	0.0 per cent	2.1 per cent	36.7 per cent
	No	Count	14	58	24	95	113	304
		per cent of Total	2.9 per cent	12.1 per cent	5.0 per cent	19.8 per cent	23.5 per cent	63.3 per cent
Total		**Count**	**88**	**142**	**32**	**95**	**123**	**480**
		per cent of Total	**18.3 per cent**	**29.6 per cent**	**6.7 per cent**	**19.8 per cent**	**25.6 per cent**	**100.0 per cent**

Chi-square value = 216.160*, DF = 4 (Significant at 5 per cent level)

As to hypotheses respondents are requested to answer in 'Yes' or 'No' response. In response to the first hypothesis that is, though

Orissa's draft resettlement and rehabilitation policy is an improvement on the national policy, it does not go far enough in ensuring adequate majors to the affected people, 36.7 per cent respondents replied in positive and remaining 63.3 per cent says no. Here the above table shows that there is a correlation occurs between the satisfaction level and the response. The X^2 value is 216.160 with Degree of Freedom 4 from the Table value 9.49 at 5 per cent level of significance. The data shows that the hypothesis is accepted and significant.

Table 6.42: Hypothesis-2

			Q6					*Total*
			Strongly Satisfied	*Adequately Satisfied*	*Undecided*	*Some how dissatisfied*	*Strongly Satisfied*	
Q19	Yes	Count	4	26	28	95	121	274
		Per cent of Total	0.8 per cent	5.4 per cent	5.8 per cent	19.8 per cent	25.2 per cent	57.1 per cent
	No	Count	84	116	4	0	2	206
		Per cent of Total	17.5 per cent	24.2 per cent	0.8 per cent	0.0 per cent	0.4 per cent	42.9 per cent
Total		**Count**	**88**	**142**	**32**	**95**	**123**	**480**
		Per cent of Total	**18.3 per cent**	**29.6 per cent**	**6.7 per cent**	**19.8 per cent**	**25.6 per cent**	**100.0 per cent**

Chi-square value = 355.399 *, DF = 4 (Significant at 5 per cent level)

The above Table shows that the Chi Square value is 355.399 with DF 4 is significant. Here the hypothesis 2 is accepted.

Table 6.43: Hypothesis-3

			Q6					*Total*
			Strongly Satisfied	*Adequately Satisfied*	*Undecided*	*Some how dissatisfied*	*Strongly Satisfied*	
Q20	Yes	Count	4	20	28	93	119	264
		Per cent of Total	0.8 per cent	4.2 per cent	5.8 per cent	19.4 per cent	24.8 per cent	55.0 per cent
	No	Count	84	122	4	2	4	216
		Per cent of Total	17.5 per cent	25.4 per cent	0.8 per cent	0.4 per cent	0.8 per cent	45.0 per cent
Total		**Count**	**88**	**142**	**32**	**95**	**123**	**480**
		Per cent of Total	**18.3 per cent**	**29.6 per cent**	**6.7 per cent**	**19.8 per cent**	**25.6 per cent**	**100.0 per cent**

Table No-6.44 Hypothesis-4

			Q6					
			Strongly Satisfied	*Adequately Satisfied*	*Undecided*	*Some how dissatisfied*	*Strongly Satisfied*	*Total*
Q21	Yes	Count	4	22	24	95	113	258
		Per cent of Total	0.8 per cent	4.6 per cent	5.0 per cent	19.8 per cent	23.5 per cent	53.8 per cent
	No	Count	84	120	8	0	10	222
		Per cent of Total	17.5 per cent	25.0 per cent	1.7 per cent	0.0 per cent	2.1 per cent	46.2 per cent
Total		**Count**	**88**	**142**	**32**	**95**	**123**	**480**
		Per cent of Total	**18.3 per cent**	**29.6 per cent**	**6.7 per cent**	**19.8 per cent**	**25.6 per cent**	**100.0 per cent**

Chi-square value = 328.762*, DF = 4 (Significant at 5 per cent level)

The above two hypotheses as put in Table 6.43, 6.44 are also accepted with the X^2 value 357.458 and 328.762, DF 4 is significant at 5 per cent level of significance respectively.

In fact, the fitness of goodness of the hypotheses are put in the Table No.6.45 for better appreciation.

Table 6.45: Testing of Hypotheses: An Overview

Hypotheses	*Level of significance*	*Calculated Value*	*Remark*
1. Though Orissa's draft resettlement and rehabilitation policy is an improvement on the national policy, it does not go far enough in ensuring adequate majors to the affected people.	0.05	216.160[a] DF=4	**Accepted**
2. The development-induced –displacement process is leading to widening the gap between the rich and poor.	0.05	355.399[a] DF = 4	**Accepted**
3. The present pattern of development is the continuing powerlessness of the weaker sections due to displacement and without any benefits from these development projects.	0.05	357.458[a] DF = 4	**Accepted**
4. The Rehabilitation policy promises for the betterment of ousters but actually the effect is impoverishment, landlessness, joblessness, food insecurity, loss of common property and increased mortality.	0.05	328.762 DF = 4	**Accepted**

The result of Hypotheses testing is placed in figure 6.8.

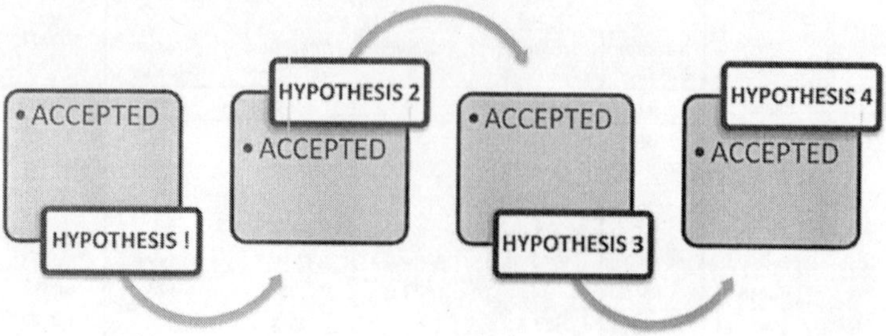

Figure 6.8

Chapter 7

A Final Word

India has invested in industrial projects, dams, roads, mines, power plants and new cities to achieve rapid economic growth. Available reports indicate that more than 21 million people are internally displaced populations (IDPs) due to development projects in India although the tribal population only makes up eight per cent of the total population, more than 40 per cent of the development induced displaced are tribal peoples in India. The difficulties faced by IDPs are numerous but distinct. Their right to participate and contest in the political processes is difficult. Such consequences lead to the requirement of legislations that address not only the issue of compensation, but also of resettlement, rehabilitation and participation in negotiation. Hence, the objectives of the study are to bring forth the impacts of major development projects on Internally Displaced Populations in India. It cannot be denied that development induced displacement has been an ancient phenomenon. Development projects are mostly targeted towards river systems, mines, forests etc. Moreover, the segment of population which is widely affected is the tribal population which is already a deprived segment in the Indian society. However, displacement became plight of the people and came under notice in post-independence era especially after first dam was constructed under Narmada Valley Development Project. The consequences of displacement are wide and varied. The displacement causes profound economic hardships. Compensation which is assured for the internally displaced population is meagre and hardly suffices to the need of those displaced. There is no infrastructure so to say; there is hardly any opportunity towards income generation. By their high frequency, cumulative magnitude, and destructive socio-economic and cultural effects, forced displacements have come to be recognised as a severe pathology of development, of growing concern and visibility on international and national agendas. In India, development projects will continue in the years to come. Hence, Indian government should frame a strategy so as to reduce if not eradicate the hardships of those displaced as a result of development projects. There is hardly any nation-wide framework on the issue of internal displacement. The government's response to IDP due to development projects is largely vague, and the displaced are therefore often left unnoticed. Hence, there is an urgent need for the government undertakes surveys in affected areas in order to document the magnitude of the problem and to develop a policy for a consistent nation-wide approach for assistance and protection of internally displaced populations. The Government should also strengthen its institutional capacity to assist IDPs. Affected populations should benefit directly and sustainably from the project forcing them off their land. The displaced population should be actively involved while framing the rehabilitation packages. Provision of new land should be the cornerstone of the rehabilitation policy.

Development projects have been projected as the benefit for the society and economy of the nation and the state. Whenever development projects are undertaken, the people living in the project area of whose lands are acquired for the project have to pay an extra price, in terms of loss of their lands of livelihood. There is an attempt to justify it as a cost of development, and to project it as an opportunity to improve the living condition of the indigenous people. However, the state government's support for different development projects has created inequities, social unrest and instability in the society. In a democratic context, the systematic dispossession of tribal people's rights through officially ordained force is totally undemocratic and unacceptable. The uses of force or coercion against economically backward people in Niyamgiri, Kalingnagar, or Kashipur unwilling to change have to be discarded. The benefits which may increase in an area pursuant to change and establishment of a project shall be deemed to be due to the larger community rather than individuals, groups or corporate bodies. The development induced displacement should be minimised and if possible avoided. If at all there is a

negotiated form of compensation proves not to be the most appropriate or effective option, PAPs tend to feel more satisfied.

There is an inverse relationship between scale of displacement and extent of achieving successful resettlement outcomes even in countries with best policy, institutional capacity and political commitment to do proper resettlement. There are a few good examples of minimising displacement. Generally, participation of the affected people has been superficial or treated as unimportant by those responsible for the project. Real participation implies the capacity to influence or even modify decisions. In several countries, the indigenous and tribal peoples displaced by large dams seem to have experienced higher levels of landlessness, unemployment, indebtedness, and hunger. The studies have also documented the adverse impact of displacement on women and children. Only situations where loss of land and access to natural resources were replaced with sustainable resources women had opportunities to recover their social and economic worth and respect. Some of the specific dominant themes emerging from displacement literature are:

- The displaced and affected people rarely received complete and authentic information on the dam project, the nature and extent of displacement and other negative impacts, and R&R provisions;
- absence of baseline surveys and inability to determine number of people displaced and affected: the displaced and affected people normally did not have any role in generation of baseline information, development of resettlement plans, or their implementation and monitoring;
- traumatic forced and delayed relocation; denial of development opportunity for years, and often decades, due to long displacement process;
- problems (related to infrastructure, relationship with host communities, etc.) in resettlement sites;
- loss of livelihood of people living downstream not properly assessed and compensated.

A successful resettlement with development is a fundamental

commitment and responsibility of the State. No development project can result in complete alienation of the rights, customary and legal, of people through payment of a one-time compensation or facilitated relocation. On the contrary, the process must result in the creation of new rights that will render people direct beneficiaries of the development project. Just as displacement is not an inevitable consequence of infrastructure development, resettlement need not necessarily result in impoverishment. Central to positive resettlement and rehabilitation will be the empowering of people, particularly the economically and socially marginalised as a result of both the process and outcomes of resettlement with development.

Against this background attempt has been made to portray the whole picture of the thesis. In this thesis the avowed objectives of the study are to analyse the basic concept of Displacement and Rehabilitation in Indian context; to focus on the implications and problems relating to the problems with special measures to strengthen it; to place an opinion study of the respondents and to provide a concluding remark as to indicating suggestive improvements in the area. The following objectives are placed below:

- To analyse the major factors lead to displacement and its positive and negative impacts.
- To examine the prevalence of the Rehabilitation policies work.
- To focus and analyse the steps taken by the government for the resettlement of the displaced people.
- To explore the impact of globalisation and liberalisation on the industrial development and displacement.
- To place an opinion study of respondents.
- To provide a concluding remark on the rehabilitation policy in India indicating suggestive improvements in the area.

Further to support the analysis the following hypotheses are taken.

- Though Orissa's draft resettlement and rehabilitation policy is an improvement on the national policy, it does not go far enough in ensuring adequate majors to the affected people.

- Though the displaced families are given some monetary compensation but the issue of socially meaningful rehabilitation is bypassed in the name of modernisation.
- The development-induced –displacement process is leading to widening the gap between the rich and poor.
- The present pattern of development is the continuing powerlessness of the weaker sections due to displacement and without any benefits from these development projects.
- The Rehabilitation policy promises for the betterment of ousters but actually the effect is impoverishment, landlessness, joblessness, food insecurity, loss of common property and increased mortality.

For this the scholar used traditional as well as scientific methods for the analysis. Moreover to be specific the scholar has used questionnaire and survey method for collecting primary data. The data so collected from 400 respondents is analysed with the use of statistical techniques such as Correlation and Chi Square Test. No doubt the result has an important bearing on the four square analysis of the coveted problem. It is needless to say that for collection of data stratified random sampling techniques has been used. Besides to fortify the analysis part, the scholar has reviewed a good number of books, journals, reports and research studies.

In fact Displacement and Rehabilitation is a vast subject with multi-dimensional ramifications. To deal with that the whole gamut of the study is divided into 5 chapters, beside introduction and conclusion.

In the second chapter the basic ideas about the Development induced Displacement analysis have been discussed and the study gives conceptual clarity about topic from theoretical point of view.

In the third chapter the historical background is also analysed. Here the scholar puts light on the displacement cases of Odisha. It studies the industrial development projects of Odisha.

The fourth chapter deals with the problems of displacement affected peoples. It studies the post-displacement effect on their life style.

The fifth chapter puts light on the Rehabilitation Policy and strategies for the development of the concerned people.

This sixth chapter is totally based on the data provided by the respondents. Moreover, it is an analytical study of various data so collected. To be specific here conclusions are drawn on analysing the data as to the study from various angles.

Major Findings

Before coming to a final conclusion, it is pertinent here to place the major findings of the study. Out of 500 respondents 480 respondents have the knowledge of the term rehabilitation. Rest of the 20 questionnaires has to be rejected due to lack of knowledge. 42.1 per cent of people from age group 31-40 are more affected by the Rehabilitation policy. Male persons are comparatively more affected than female members. Married person represents 90 per cent out of 480 respondents. The study based on a stratified random sampling method. Maximum number around 59.6 per cent people up to 10th are affected by displacement. The below 2000-5000 income groups are more vulnerable in comparison to other income group. 43.3 per cent of the total respondents are ST population and they are worst affected by the faulty rehabilitation policy.

Pearson method of Chi Square Test has been used to test the fitness of hypotheses with the use of SPSS 20.0 software. These are placed below for better clarity:

- Though Orissa's draft resettlement and rehabilitation policy is an improvement on the national policy, it does not go far enough in ensuring adequate majors to the affected people.
- Though the displaced families are given some monetary compensation but the issue of socially meaningful rehabilitation is bypassed in the name of modernisation.
- The development-induced –displacement process is leading to widening the gap between the rich and poor.
- The present pattern of development is the continuing powerlessness of the weaker sections due to displacement and without any benefits from these development projects.
- The Rehabilitation policy promises for the betterment of ousters but actually the effect is impoverishment,

landlessness, joblessness, food insecurity, loss of common property and increased mortality.

As per the data analysis all of the above hypotheses are accepted.

Thus, in recent years rehabilitation and resettlement of project affected families has turned out to be the most vital and sensitive issue for the development projects, either it be Kalinga Nagar in Jajpur or POSCO in Jagatsinghpur, Singur in West Bengal Different development projects are being opposed by the inhabitants of these areas and being delayed because of the opposition from the PAFs (Project Affected Families). This has been primarily due to the bitter R&R (Resettlement and Rehabilitation) experience of PAFs. In the post independence period, the development projects deemed to be temples of progress, ultimately turned out to be "graveyards" for millions of these PAFs. Although these projects did bring development but the cost has been enormous. There is no denial of the fact that if the quality of life of people is to be improved, development projects are a must but there is general consensus now that development should not be at the cost of people and their environment, while the social activists and the academicians have put the issue of R&R on the national agenda.

Index